P9-DNR-836

Oskar Schindler

**Holocaust Heroes
and Nazi Criminals**

Oskar Schindler

Saving Jews From the Holocaust

Ann Byers

Enslow Publishers, Inc.

40 Industrial Road   PO Box 38
Box 398   Aldershot
Berkeley Heights, NJ 07922   Hants GU12 6BP
USA   UK
http://www.enslow.com

To Steve, who after thirty-five years is still
my stability, my strength, and my joy.

Copyright © 2005 by Ann Byers

Library of Congress Cataloging-in-Publication Data:

Byers, Ann.
    Oskar Schindler : saving Jews from the Holocaust / Ann Byers.
       p. cm. — (Holocaust heroes and Nazi criminals)
    Includes bibliographical references and index.
    ISBN-10: 0-7660-2534-9
      1. Schindler, Oskar, 1908–1974—Juvenile literature. 2. Righteous Gentiles in the
Holocaust—Juvenile literature. 3. Righteous Gentiles—Biography—Juvenile literature.
4. Holocaust, Jewish (1939–1945)—Juvenile literature.
5. World War, 1939–1945—Jews—Rescue—Juvenile literature. I. Title.
II. Series.
    D804.66.S38B94 2005
    940.53′1835′092—dc22

                                         2004019061

ISBN-13: 978-0-7660-2534-9

Printed in the United States of America

10 9 8 7 6 5 4 3 2

To Our Readers: We have done our best to make sure all Internet Addresses in this book
were active and appropriate when we went to press. However, the author and the publisher
have no control over and assume no liability for the material available on those Internet
sites or on other Web sites they may link to. Any comments or suggestions can be sent by
e-mail to comments@enslow.com or to the address on the back cover.

Illustration Credits: Bud Tullin, courtesy of USHMM Photo Archives, p. 141 (top); Enslow
Publishers, Inc., p. 16; James Sanders, courtesy of the USHMM Photo Archives, p. 142 (top);
National Archives and Records Administration, pp. 23, 31, 47, 51, 99, 112, 118, 137 (third
from top), 140 (bottom); National Museum of Auschwitz-Birkenau, Courtesy of USHMM,
p. 76; State Archives of the Russian Federation, courtesy of USHMM, p. 140 (top); USHMM,
pp. 54, 130, 137 (second from bottom), 139 (top), 142 (bottom); USHMM, courtesy of
Archiwum Panstwowe w Krakowie, p. 57; USHMM, courtesy of Avi Granot, pp. 60, 122;
USHMM, courtesy of the Israel Government Press Office, p. 105; USHMM, courtesy of Jack
Sutin, p. 73; USHMM, courtesy of Leopold Page Photographic Collection, pp. 5, 7, 8, 11, 14,
26, 29, 40, 45, 78, 93, 109, 126, 133, 137 (top), 143, 151, 154, 157, 158; USHMM, courtesy of
Lorenz Schmuhl, pp. 49, 137 (third from bottom), 138 (top); USHMM, courtesy of Main
Commission for the Prosecution of the Crimes against the Polish Nation, pp. 38, 71, 80, 137
(second from top), 138 (bottom); USHMM, courtesy of the National Museum of American
Jewish History, pp. 137 (bottom), 139 (bottom), 141 (bottom).

Cover Illustration: USHMM, courtesy of Avi Granot; USHMM, courtesy of Lorenz Schmuhl
(background)

Contents

Acknowledgments

The deeds of Oskar Schindler are known only because of one man's dogged determination that they would be. The world owes a debt of gratitude to Poldek Pfefferberg, also known as Leopold Page, for insisting that the story be told. I am grateful also to Thomas Keneally and Steven Spielberg for bringing Schindler's story to a wider audience. I am indebted to the many Schindlerjuden who, when asked, recounted their own parts of the story. I know that remembering meant reliving great pain. I am deeply thankful for Maren Read of the United States Holocaust Memorial Museum. Maren helped me find wonderful photographs and obtain permission to use them. All these people have helped keep alive a true story that continues to inspire.

Fast Facts About Oskar Schindler

Born April 28, 1908, in Zwittau, then a part of the Austrian Empire; died October 9, 1974, in Frankfurt, West Germany.

Lived in Austro-Hungarian Empire, Czechoslovakia, Poland, Germany, and Argentina.

Worked for the German Intelligence Service (Abwehr) as a spy from 1935.

Lived in Krakow, Poland from the time immediately after Germany took over that country in September 1939 until October 1944.

Purchased and operated Deutsche Emailwaren Fabrik (Emalia), a factory that produced enamel kitchenware and armaments. Because of war contracts, cheap labor, and black-market sales, made a fortune from this operation.

Arrested three times: (1) On suspicion of black-market dealing, (2) for allegedly kissing a Jewish girl, and (3) on suspicion of conspiring with or bribing Plaszow commandant Amon Goeth to aid Jews.

Made reports about the treatment of Jews in Poland to the American Joint Distribution Committee, a Jewish welfare organization that distributed money to alleviate the suffering of Jewish people. Distributed funds for that organization.

Operated a forced-labor camp from spring 1943 until the end of the war in April 1945, first outside Krakow, Poland then in Brinnlitz in German-occupied Czechoslovakia.

Supported after the war by the American Joint Distribution Committee and gifts from Jews he saved.

Lived in Argentina from 1949 to 1957, operating a nutria ranch.

Gave testimony against some of the personnel of Plaszow.

Spent an estimated 4 million Reichsmarks saving at least twelve thousand Jews: buying food, medicine, and other items; building two camps to shelter them; and bribing officials.

Honored by Yad Vashem as a Righteous Gentile.

Introduction:
A Righteous Gentile

The visit was a surprise. Of course SS officers could make an inspection anytime they chose. Germany, under the leadership of Adolf Hitler and his Nazi political party, had conquered Poland, and the soldier-police of his SS could do anything they wanted. They were the enforcement arm of the Nazi rule in occupied Poland. Yet it was still always a surprise when they came.

It was only logical that the SS would come to the enamelware factory. This was a business that had government contracts. The SS checked up on companies that manufactured goods for the government. Besides, the factory employed a number of Jews. There were laws, written and unwritten, about what Jews could and could not do, where Jews could and could not be, how Jews should and should not be treated. These SS men made it their mission to enforce those laws.

Whenever an inspection team came, the factory workers assumed the same pose. They stayed at their work stations and kept their eyes down. The important thing was not to be noticed. To stand out was to be singled out. No one wanted to be singled out by the SS.

Even with their eyes down, the laborers knew that their *Direktor* was with the inspectors. Many said they could smell him before they saw him. They could detect the fragrance of his cologne well before he entered the factory floor. Oskar Schindler was a wealthy man, and he doused himself in expensive cologne every morning. The workers also knew *Herr Direktor* was in the room by the aroma of his ever-present cigarette. He was a chain smoker and he always had cigarettes, even though they were hard to obtain in war-torn

Poland. Some said they could tell he was coming not by his colognes and cigarettes, but by the glint of sunlight reflected off his huge diamond ring.

However they knew, they breathed a little easier. With Herr Schindler present, the SS men would be somewhat restrained. Nevertheless, the workers kept their heads down and their guards up. One of their number, however, had forgotten the do-not-stand-out rule. Old Lamus was outside, all by himself, painfully obvious, trudging slowly across the factory yard pushing a wheelbarrow ahead of him.

The inspectors stopped, intrigued by the lone figure. Everything about him was wrong. For one thing, he was obviously too old to be here. For the past year these very men had combed the Jewish section of Krakow again and again, looking for people such as this. Nearly everyone older than fifty or younger than fourteen had been removed. Only those Jews of economic use to Germany had been allowed to live. How had this man survived this long?

He had survived because Oskar Schindler had falsified his age. The SS did not know, of course, but several of the men and women in this factory were as much as ten or twenty years older than the company records showed. Schindler had also falsified occupations in order to bring people to the relative safety of his plant. Men like Lamus carted goods across the yard because they had no other skills.

The old man was obviously not fit for work. His gait was slow and his head was bowed. He could barely push the wheelbarrow. In the Nazi mind, Jews were less than human, not deserving of life. To the SS, this one had no redeeming quality whatsoever. "Why is he so sad?," one inspector asked.

The answer should have been obvious. Until just a few weeks ago thousands of Jews still lived in Krakow. They had been confined to a tiny ghetto, crowded and filthy, but they were alive. Then the SS had invaded the Jewish quarters, demolishing homes, killing wantonly without reason. Everyone at the factory had lost loved ones when the ghetto was cleared. Lamus had lost his wife and only child.

No tear came to the eye of the SS commander when he heard the explanation. This was a Jew; neither he nor his family was of any importance to the Nazis who ruled Poland now. He turned to his aide and told him to shoot the Jew "so that he might be reunited with his family in heaven."[1] Then he laughed loudly and walked on, leaving his assistant to carry out his order.

The commander apparently meant this to be a public execution. That way the Jews on the floor would see what was done to any who were unproductive. He evidently wanted all of them, these people who refused to look at him, to know what their eventual fate would be. And he wanted the aide to be very comfortable with killing Jews: *en masse*, in large groups, as in the emptying of the ghetto or one at a time as with this dejected old man.

The SS aide had no qualms about killing a Jew. People did not rise to his position by being squeamish about shooting civilians. He ordered the frightened Lamus to slip his pants down to his ankles. It was not enough for the Nazis to murder defenseless Jews; they had to humiliate them also. The aide commanded Lamus to begin walking across the yard, dragging his pants after him. SS men seldom shot a person who was

Oskar Schindler poses with his horse on the grounds of the Emalia enamelworks in Krakow. Schindler was wealthy and often bribed Nazis in order to save Jews.

facing them. The preferred method of execution was a bullet in the back of the neck. Lamus shuffled obediently toward the far side of the yard, resigned to his death.

Herr Direktor tried to sound like a company executive whose business practices were being questioned. "You are interfering with all my discipline here!" he complained. "The morale of my workers will suffer!"[2] Surely the inspector realized that the factory was prosperous because Schindler knew how to run it. Schindler implied that he could teach the man to do better. Many times he had bragged that he knew how to get work out of Jews.

But the aide only sneered. Discipline was his business, and he performed it with a gun. He took out his pistol. Desperately Schindler cried, "Production for *der Vaterland* [the Fatherland] will be affected!"[3] It was the argument to which he always resorted. His was an essential business, producing necessary items for the German army. Any disruption in his factory would cause the soldiers at the front to suffer. The SS aide, however, apparently did not see the connection between enamelware production, this old man, and Germany's chance of winning the war.

Herr Direktor cast aside all attempt at reason. He appealed instead to the officer's baser nature. Totally abandoning any pretext of indifference, he shouted, "A bottle of schnapps if you don't shoot him!"[4] The aide stopped, his pistol in midair. He smiled. Schindler quickly took his arm, forced a smile on his own face, and led the man to his office. He kept his store of liquor there for just such occasions.

Thus the German factory owner bought the life of a single Jew with a bottle of liquor. Lamus was but one of many people kept alive through the nightmare of the Holocaust by Oskar Schindler.

The Jewish nation of Israel has a name for non-Jews who saved some of their people from the genocide during World War II: Righteous Among the Nations. These people are also sometimes called Righteous Gentiles. The designation of Righteous Gentile is not given lightly. The gentile must have rescued helpless Jews who would otherwise have died or been sent to concentration camps. The rescuer had to know that the act of helping a Jew was done at risk of death. And the gentile could not receive any payment or reward for the help given.[5] In Israel, Righteous Gentiles are considered great heroes.

Of the 20,205 people who have been declared Righteous Among the Nations, Oskar Schindler is an unlikely hero. From his youth until the end of the war, he was a member of the Nazi party. As an industrialist, he became rich by exploiting Jewish labor. In his extravagant, self-centered lifestyle, he probably broke every one of the Ten Commandments many times over. Yet he spent his entire fortune, perhaps 4 million German marks, to rescue Jews. He was arrested three times and risked death every day. In the end, he saved more than twelve hundred Jewish lives.

1

The Adventurer

Some called it "the war to end all wars." And many people thought, or at least hoped, that the Great War would indeed be the last major conflict in Europe. But the truth was the war, which would later be called World War I, created as many problems as it ended. The fighting intensified the bad feelings between people of different ethnic groups. In 1914, before the conflict, central Europe had been divided among dozens of ethnic and national groups. The war changed some of the boundary lines between countries, but the hostility between the different groups remained.

Nowhere was the situation worse than in the provinces of Bohemia and Moravia. Before the war, these provinces in the heart of Europe were part of the Austro-Hungarian Empire. They were home to Czechs, Germans, and Jews. In the area around the Sudeten Mountains, Germans far outnumbered Czechs, the next largest group. This meant that, in the Sudetenland Germans had the best jobs and the most privileges. But the Treaty of Versailles that ended the war carved up the Austro-Hungarian Empire into four separate countries. Bohemia and Moravia became part of the new country of Czechoslovakia. Overnight the Sudeten Germans went from being the majority in an Austrian province to a minority in a new state. They made up only 22 percent of the population of Czechoslovakia.

The Schindler Family

Born on April 28, 1908, Oskar Schindler was ten years old when World War I ended in 1918. The Schindlers were German by ethnicity and lived in Moravia, which had become part of Czechoslovakia. The political change had little immediate effect on Oskar's family. His father, Hans, owned a farm machinery company, and Czechs as well as Germans needed farm equipment. So the family prospered. Oskar lived comfortably in a large, two-story home surrounded by beautiful gardens. It was in a middle-class neighborhood of the city of Zwittau (in the Czech language, Svitavy) where he was born.

Zwittau was an industrial city. Its mills produced steel, textiles, and all kinds of equipment. It was an important center of transportation, a railroad junction city. Trains carried its goods to Germany, Poland, and other parts of Czechoslovakia. Zwittau also had a diverse population. Although predominately German, it was also home to some gypsies and a number of German-speaking Jews. Oskar's next-door neighbor was a modern-thinking, well-educated rabbi. Oskar went to school with the rabbi's two sons.

The schools Oskar attended were German institutions. Most of the Sudetenland had remained German, and the German-speaking people had kept their schools. With his sister Elfriede, who was six years younger, Oskar and

his Jewish neighbors went to the German grammar school. Oskar was enrolled in the science courses. His father's plan was that he become an engineer. He needed to learn the technical aspects of manufacturing because his father expected him to take over the family business.

Oskar's father had been an insurance salesman, but his insurance business had gone bankrupt. He was naturally mechanical, so making machines interested him. He went into business manufacturing and selling tractors, electric generators, and other pieces of farm equipment. His company did well. Hans Schindler was gone much of the time, buying materials for his firm and selling its products.

While his father was away from home, Oskar's mother pampered him. Francesca Louisa Schindler, or Fannie as people called her, was very different from his father. Hans Schindler was coarse and unschooled; Fannie Schindler was cultured and educated. He was loud and outgoing; she was quiet and reserved. He liked to drink and party; she preferred to go to church.

Adolescence

When he was home, Hans Schindler was also guilty of spoiling his only son. He knew that Oskar was interested in motorcycles. The boy loved going fast. He loved the thrill, the adventure of racing. It was about the only thing that offered any excitement in Zwittau in the 1920s. Once he built his own motorbike out of spare parts. When Oskar was in high

Top: In Krakow, Poland, rail lines connected the Plaszow concentration camp to the vast camp system that stretched across Nazi-occupied Europe. Bottom: A map of present-day Poland, showing the location of important cities.

school, his father presented him a motorcycle as a gift. It was an Italian make, very big and very powerful. It was fire red in color and red hot in speed. Oskar sped everywhere on it, the envy of all his classmates.

Before long, Oskar was racing motorcycles. Several of the factories of Zwittau had racing teams, and Oskar was on the team of his father's factory. His father had bought him another motorcycle. This one was smaller, lighter, built for the sharp curves of the mountain races. It, too, was Italian, also red, and even less common than the first one. That one had been a toy; this one was for winning prizes. In his first race, Oskar came in third. It was enough to put him on the circuit, competing with riders far more experienced.

His second race was even more exciting. He was pitted against some of the best men and machines in Europe. Within an hour he was near the front of the pack. In what he thought was the final lap, he passed the leaders and crossed the finish line ahead of everyone else. But his victory was short-lived. Somehow he had miscalculated. He thought the contest was over, but he actually had another lap to go. By the time he realized his mistake and revved his engine again, others had caught up and overtaken him. He finished fourth.

Although Oskar might have liked to devote all his energy to play, he was becoming a young man, and work was claiming more of his time. He had to learn all the details of the family business. In addition to managing the manufacturing operation, the heir to the company needed to be able to sell its wares. Hans Schindler took his son with him on his out-of-town sales trips.

Emilie

One of those trips took him to the Bohemian countryside, to the farming village of Alt-Molstein. In that village, father and son stopped at the Pelzl farm. While Hans Schindler described the benefits of his products to Herr Pelzl, Oskar did not speak. He may have been learning how to make a sales pitch, but he did not take his eyes off Herr Pelzl's daughter Emilie. She was beautiful and gentle, much like his mother. Like his mother, she had been educated, first in Catholic schools, then in an agricultural institute. She was, again like his mother, very religious.

Just as Oskar was drawn to this farmer's daughter, Emilie was impressed with Oskar. She saw him as tall and thin "with broad shoulders, blond hair, and deep blue eyes."[1] He seemed dignified and confident, and a little mysterious. He and his father made several visits to Alt-Molstein, and every time Emilie became more intrigued with this handsome young man. Although she tried to ignore him, she later said, "I always felt his deep blue eyes caressing me. It was a virile [strong] look, dark and penetrating, that I could not get out of my mind."[2] Emilie did not resist Oskar's good looks and charm for very long. Within just a few weeks of their first meeting, his passionate kisses and embraces had won her over. They talked of marriage.

Winning her father's blessing, however, was another matter. Emilie was his only daughter, and his only son also was ready to leave home. Oskar would take her away from their little village. Herr Pelzl did not know Oskar well, and he did not trust this smooth-talking city boy. He appeared too wild, too young, and in too much of a rush. However, Emilie was in love, so her father reluctantly agreed to the marriage. He promised Oskar a dowry of one hundred thousand Czech crowns.

Oskar's father was just as unhappy as Emilie's father with the quick courtship. His own marriage was not particularly happy, and he feared the same for his son. Emilie was much like his wife: docile, naive, and entirely too religious in his view. And Oskar was very much like him. He followed his feelings rather than reason, sought pleasure rather than security, and often acted without considering the consequences. He was too undisciplined and self-centered to settle down with just one woman.

But in the end, Hans Schindler also gave in to his son's infatuation. Oskar and Emilie were married in March 1928, in an inn on the edge of Zwittau. They were both twenty years old. They had known each other for only six months. Amongst the many guests, the bride and groom made a striking picture. He looked elegant, almost aristocratic, the model of Aryan strength. She was lovely in her short white dress and long white veil. Her grandmother told everyone, over and over, that she "looked like Sleeping Beauty, just awakened from her long sleep by a handsome prince."[3]

The Sybarite

The fairy tale was not to last long. Instead of whisking his bride to his castle, Oskar took her to his parents' house. For the first few years of their lives together, Oskar and Emilie lived on the second floor and Hans and Fannie lived on the floor below. Emilie spent her days helping her mother-in-law, who was ill and often in bed. She spent her evenings arguing with her father-in-law. She was glad when they finally moved to their own house.

Even in their own home, however, the fairy tale was clouded. Emilie found that Oskar was truly a prince in some ways. He was kind and gentle. Always happy, he made their life together fun. And above all else, he was extremely generous. He bought his wife expensive gifts. He filled their house with beautiful furnishings and crystal chandeliers.

He sent her flowers often. However, in other ways, he was a great disappointment. He spent money carelessly. He drank more than she thought he should. And he stayed out very late at night, frequently with women.

When Emilie's father found out about Oskar's romantic adventures, he refused to pay him the remainder of the dowry he had promised. He had already given him a portion of the wedding payment, and Oskar had used it to buy a deluxe automobile. He loved the look and feel of being rich.

When Emilie complained about his spending or his womanizing, Oskar always had the same answer. He said she was too serious, too tight-fisted, and too inhibited. She held herself back, missing out on excitement. He, on the other hand, considered himself fun-loving, liberal, and unrestrained. He lived life to the fullest, enjoying all the sensual pleasures it offered. He told her she was an ascetic—a person who denied herself everything—and he was a sybarite—someone who denied himself nothing.

Seventy years later, history would describe Oskar Schindler in exactly the same way. One of the people he rescued recalled that he "liked three W's—wealth, women, and whiskey."[4] Another remembered him as "a bit of a playboy."[5] Both said, however, that his genial nature gave them hope in the face of unspeakable hardships: "He always smiled, he was always optimistic, a ray of light at the end of the tunnel."[6] Oskar Schindler took from life everything he wanted, but he also gave generously.

The Depression

The early 1930s were years of taking and giving. Soon after he was married, Oskar Schindler embarked on an adventure that was not of his choosing. As a young male citizen of Czechoslovakia, he served in the country's army. As might be expected, the pampered son of a well-to-do merchant did not like military life. As soon as his term of service ended, he returned to Zwittau, to his father's company.

But Zwittau was different in the 1930s. The depression that had engulfed the entire world had taken its toll on the mountain city and on the Schindler business. No one had money to spend on tractors or generators for their farms. In 1935 Hans Schindler was forced to close his factory. Along with millions of people worldwide, Oskar was unemployed.

He did not remain idle for long, however. His outgoing personality, his skill in selling, and some of the contacts he had made through his father helped him find a job. While most of Europe was out of work, Oskar Schindler became sales manager for Moravian Electrotechnic Company. It was a position that required him to travel. It took him throughout Czechoslovakia and across the border into Poland. And that life on the road opened up the possibility of a new and dangerous adventure.

The Nazi

Even before the great depression hit Germany, the country was in ruins economically. The Great War, as World War I was called then, had devastated the land. The government had poured its wealth into guns, bombs, and fighter planes. Most of these had been used up or destroyed. Many cities had been reduced to rubble. The war had cost Germany 164 billion marks ($41 billion).[1] Recovering would cost billions more.

In addition to the expenses of rebuilding its shattered land, Germany had another burden. The victorious nations had insisted that Germany pay what it had cost them to fight the war. The Allies also wanted reparations, payment for what it would cost to repair the damage they had suffered as a result of the war. They set the figure for reparations at $33 billion, to be paid in gold, not paper money.

Even if the figure had been a fraction of that amount, Germany could not pay. The war had emptied the country's treasuries and the peace treaty had nearly destroyed the nation's ability to produce any income. The Allies had stripped Germany of more than 10 percent of its territory; land that contained the coal and iron it needed to restart its economy. Without raw materials, the country had no wealth. German money was worthless. At the end of the war, four German marks could buy one dollar's worth of goods; by November 1923, it took four billion marks to purchase the same amount of merchandise.[2]

The hopeless economic situation was only part of Germany's distress in the 1930s. The country was also bankrupt psychologically. In the Treaty of Versailles, the Allies had forced Germany to accept total blame for the war. The victorious nations further humiliated Germany by reducing the size of its army. This country, so proud of its centuries-old military tradition, could have no more than one hundred thousand soldiers. Its navy was limited to six small ships, and tanks and planes were strictly forbidden.

The Sudeten Nazi Party

Millions of demoralized, unemployed Germans turned for hope to the National Socialist German Workers' (Nazi) Party. This group promised to restore to Germany its former honor and glory. Its charismatic leader, Adolf Hitler, rallied the masses around his pledge to unite all Germans, including those in Austria and Czechoslovakia, in a Greater Germany. When Hitler became Chancellor in 1933, he ushered in what he claimed would be the nation's third great empire: the Third Reich.

Sentiment for the Nazi party was strong among Germans who lived in lands that were no longer part of Germany. The Sudetenland, in the new country of Czechoslovakia, was home to three million German-speaking people. In 1933 Konrad Henlein formed the Patriotic Front of Sudeten

Germans, a Nazi party committed to the return of the Sudetenland to Germany.

Many Germans in Czechoslovakia joined Henlein's party, including Oskar Schindler. Most signed up because of political conviction, but for Schindler it was a business decision. He was a salesman, and salesmen needed to form good relationships with potential buyers. Many of those buyers supported the Nazi goal of a Greater Germany that would include the Sudetenland.

Over his wife's objections, Oskar Schindler paid the party dues and officially became a Nazi. This entitled him to wear the Nazi swastika. Some party members wore small pins, but Oskar, ever flamboyant, had a pin the size of a large coin. For a few months he dutifully attended the party meetings. Before long, however, he found other things to do with his money and his time. He had the badge, and that was all he really needed.[3]

The swastika pin brought Schindler more than financial opportunities. All who saw it assumed that its wearer was fiercely loyal to Germany. One who noticed Schindler's emblem was Ilsa Pelikanova, a woman he met during his business travels. Schindler did not know that she worked for the *Abwehr*, the German Intelligence Service. The *Abwehr* was Hitler's spy agency.

Spy for Germany

Ilsa used Oskar's three loves—wealth, women, and whiskey—to lure him into her business. She invited him to a party where she introduced him to Eberhard Gebauer, an *Abwehr* officer. Over drinks, Gebauer explained that the young salesman had much to offer the Fatherland. He could travel to businesses and military installations in Poland and through-out Czechoslovakia without suspicion. He could simply say

Oskar Schindler and his father Hans enjoy Schindler's car outside their home in Czechoslovakia.

he was visiting his company's clients. Schindler had a friendly manner that encouraged people to talk. He seemed fearless and intelligent, able to charm his way into or out of sensitive or difficult situations. Gebauer offered Schindler a job in the foreign section of the *Abwehr*.

The pay was probably not Schindler's primary motivation for accepting the position. Patriotism or politics were small considerations.[4] However, the job's main attraction was its promise of adventure, of danger. It would feel like threading a motorcycle through the gullies and rises of the Sudeten mountains at top speed. For Schindler, even the three W's could not compare with the thrill of serious risk.

Emilie Schindler, however, never got used to the risk. She constantly worried that their activities would be discovered. Her tasks did not seem particularly dangerous. She answered the phone, ran errands, and typed reports. But it was treason for a Czechoslovak citizen to possess the information she handled every day. In addition, other spies and informers met frequently at their home. Emilie Schindler always slept fitfully, with a loaded pistol in the bedroom closet. Once she actually fired the gun in the air, after seeing a shadowy figure just outside a window.[5]

Oskar Schindler, on the other hand, loved intelligence work. There are few records to show exactly what he did in the service of Germany. One of his assignments, however, was to become very important in Hitler's plan for gaining more territory. He was able to secretly buy an army uniform from a Polish soldier. It became the pattern for one hundred fifty more Polish uniforms. The soldiers' clothes were later used to bluff the world into believing that Poland actually started what became known as World War II.

Emilie Schindler's worst fear was to become reality in July 1938. The city police came to their home. They emptied drawers, scattered papers, and tore pillows apart. They searched each room, looking behind and under everything that could be moved. The papers they were after were attached to the back of a mirror in the bedroom, hidden neatly but not well enough. The police arrested Oskar Schindler for military treason.

Counter-intelligence officials of the Republic of Czechoslovakia questioned him. According to the official report, "Under interrogation Mr. Oskar Schindler has confessed that he was in direct contact with organs [smaller groups] of the German Reich Intelligence Service (*Abwehr*), to which he was passing information."[6] Schindler could not charm his way out of this predicament. Spying was a very serious matter, and he had been caught red-handed. Hitler had been threatening to destroy Czechoslovakia, so spying for Germany was an especially serious offense. For his crime, Oskar Schindler was sentenced to death.

3

The Opportunist

Hitler's dream of restoring Germany to a glorious empire was to save Oskar Schindler's life. The Führer's call for *lebensraum*, living space, for the German people meant taking over Czechoslovakia. This he did in March 1939. When German troops entered the tiny country, German prisoners, including Schindler, were freed from Czechoslovak jails.

Hitler wanted more from Czechoslovakia than its land. He wanted its industrial wealth. Schindler watched as Hitler's armies took factories away from non-German Czechs. Those deprived of their businesses could only work for low wages for German industrialists. The Nazi way of doing business was a golden opportunity for any enterprising German.

An even greater opportunity presented itself just six months after Schindler's release from prison. Germany's invasion of Poland, which began World War II, opened up hundreds of factories to loyal Nazis. Hitler's plan for Poland was a little more complex than his blueprint for Czechoslovakia. The western part of the country was to be annexed, or joined, to Germany. The growing population of Germany was to spill over into that section. The eastern part was to be a dumping ground for people the Führer considered inferior: namely, Poles and Jews. Eventually Hitler would demand that they be expelled from eastern Poland also. Their forced removal left many openings for adventurous Germans who might come in to seek their fortunes.

Move to Krakow

And if Oskar Schindler was anything it was adventurous. About a month after Hitler took over Poland, Schindler went to this new frontier to receive orders from his superiors in the *Abwehr*. By then the Third Reich had a firm grip on Czechoslovakia and no longer needed spies there. Schindler had made a number of contacts for the agency in Poland. So he was reassigned to Krakow.

Krakow had been made the capital of the General Government, the eastern portion of German-occupied Poland. Schindler had visited the city many times in his intelligence work. He loved this place with its high medieval walls, its centuries-old Gothic castle, its gleaming twin-towered cathedral, and its ancient university. He liked the promise of its many metal, textile, and chemical factories. He decided to establish himself here and then bring his wife. He would need to purchase a house and find a business that would serve as a cover for his spying activities.

This woman in Czechoslovakia weeps as she salutes Hitler after her homeland was occupied by the Nazis.

Purchasing a house was easy. Many formerly Jewish homes were readily available, especially to someone with connections to high-ranking Nazi officials. Just weeks after Krakow fell to the Nazis on September 6, the occupying power had set about Aryanizing the General Government. That meant that all jobs, all property, and eventually all life in the country would be German. Any inferior peoples would be removed. Hitler had determined years earlier to rid his Reich of all Jews. Over the course of a year and a half, the Jews in the cities of Poland were driven from their homes. As the process of evicting Krakow's sixty thousand Jews began, Oskar and Emilie Schindler were given a beautiful apartment, luxuriously furnished, in the heart of the capital city.

Although Schindler welcomed the opportunity in Poland, he was not completely comfortable. He had been troubled by the way the Nazis had exploited the non-German people when they took over Czechoslovakia. Now the mistreatment of the Jews of Poland was even more blatant. Oskar was disturbed by his party's harshness. If the stories told years later are accurate, he searched Krakow's crowded Jewish sector until he found the family whose house he now occupied. He could not, of course, return the apartment, but he did give its former owners a generous sum of money. The family used the payment to escape into Yugoslavia.[1] These were quite likely the first Jews Oskar Schindler saved.

Powerful Connections

Schindler was less concerned with the Jews in Krakow than he was with the influential people there. For one thing, his work as an *Abwehr* agent required that he know who was who. For another, he liked being with important people. Besides, with so many changes taking place, a person never knew who might prove useful. In his first months in Poland, Oskar Schindler began to form a web of relationships.

His first contacts were with fellow Nazis. One was an officer of the SS, the military-like police agency that kept order on the streets. He would be helpful in learning about any government raids or other actions planned for the city. Another contact was an SD officer. The SD was the Security Service, the intelligence arm of the SS. This officer would know about decisions and events beyond Krakow that would affect the city. Then there were people who worked in the Armaments Inspectorate. This was the agency that decided which companies would receive contracts to manufacture goods for the army. Schindler wined and dined all the people with any power or knowledge.

And, of course, Schindler knew the *Abwehr* personnel. One of his fellow agents was a beautiful Sudeten German named Amelia.[2] She was a great help covering up anything he wished to keep hidden. She also became one of his many mistresses. He met a Polish woman, Viktoria Klonowska, who he also took often to his apartment. She introduced him to members of the Gestapo, the Nazi secret police.

Practical Connection

But Oskar Schindler needed contacts with more than powerful authorities. He also needed inside information from people on the streets. He made an invaluable connection almost by chance. It was with a twenty-seven-year-old Polish Jew named Poldek Pfefferberg.

Pfefferberg was a physical education teacher in a Krakow high school when German armies massed on the border of his country. He joined the Polish army as a lieutenant and was wounded and captured by the Nazi invaders. When the train carrying the prisoners of war stopped in

Krakow, the daring Pfefferberg convinced his guards that he was authorized to tend to his wounded comrades. Instead, the resourceful young man slipped off the train and headed to his parents' apartment. He did not know how many days or hours he had before his absence would be discovered. He had no way of knowing that within weeks his family would be removed suddenly from their home. They would be left in the December cold to find shelter wherever they could. For now, his plan was to stay as long as he felt safe, then flee south to Hungary or Rumania.

Pfefferberg and his mother were alone in her apartment when Schindler knocked on the door. Fearing the Gestapo had come to arrest him, he slipped a .22 pistol in his belt. Through a crack in the door, he could see that the visitor was a tall, well-dressed German. He told his mother to answer the knock while he hid, ready for a quick exit if necessary.

Schindler greeted Mrs. Pfefferberg courteously. "Don't worry," he began, "I'm not here to arrest anybody. I am here to make business with you."[3] He explained that he had been referred to her as an excellent decorator. He had moved into a new apartment and wanted it redecorated for his wife. Would she consider doing some work for him?

She hesitated, obviously frightened. Her son, crouching in another room, had only minutes to size up the situation. He decided to trust the polite stranger. "Listening to Schindler," he said many years later, "I knew he wasn't Gestapo. Even then I could tell he was a good man."[4] Pfefferberg buttoned his jacket over the .22, one could never trust a stranger completely, came out of hiding, and invited Schindler in.

Just as the young Jew had assessed the German, Schindler took stock of Pfefferberg. He knew that fine cloth, elegant jewelry, and even meat and rice were hard to come by in occupied Poland, especially for a Jew. Yet this family seemed to have plenty. He guessed that Pfefferberg knew where to find things and how to get them. He would need someone who could trade on the black market for him.

But he could not ask him directly. The young man would think he was police, trying to trick him. He had to ask in a way that did not threaten this potential contact. So he simply asked if Pfefferberg could buy some shirts for him like the one he was wearing. And he gave him a generous amount of cash. Within a week the two had become friends with a mutually beneficial business arrangement. The Jew supplied the Nazi with the material luxuries he wanted, and the Nazi gave the Jew enough business to keep him alive.

A New Business

Without question Schindler enjoyed material luxuries. He loved expensive suits, flashy cars, and good food and drink. To maintain his high standard of living, he needed more than his *Abwehr* salary. Just as Hitler's greedy grasp of Czechoslovakia had saved Schindler's life in March, his mercenary exploitation of Poland would make the way in December for Schindler to become rich.

Hitler had placed the General Government area of Poland in the hands of one of his lawyers, Hans Frank. As governor, Frank had two primary responsibilities: make the General Government profitable for Germany and rid the Polish region of its two and a half million Jews.[5] For the second task he had the help of Reinhard Heydrich, head of the SS Security Service (SD).

They wasted no time. Within the first two months of occupation, Frank and Heydrich had issued a series of edicts that basically turned everything Jewish over to Germans. First they took money by denying Jews access to their bank

Poldek Pfefferberg (Leopold Page)
Schindler's Black-Market Contact

Born in Krakow, Poland in 1913, Pfefferberg taught physical education in a high school in his home town. As a lieutenant in the Polish army, he fought against the Nazis. He was Schindler's contact with the black market in Krakow.

Almost one hundred members of his family perished in the Holocaust, but he and his wife Ludmila survived. After the war, they began a school for displaced children in Munich, Germany. Pfefferberg vowed that he would tell the world how Schindler saved him and twelve hundred others.

After emigrating to the United States, the couple settled in Los Angeles in 1950. They opened a shop in Beverly Hills for the sale and repair of leather goods. Any time writers, producers, or agents came into his shop, Pfefferberg told them Schindler's story and asked them to publicize it. In 1980 he told the story to Australian author Thomas Keneally, who agreed to write it.

Pfefferberg advised Keneally as he wrote and later advised Steven Spielberg as he turned the book into a film. Having fulfilled his vow, he then helped found the Oskar Schindler Humanities Foundation, which recognizes people and groups that perform heroic acts without regard to race or nationality.

Poldek Pfefferberg died on March 9, 2001. He explained his persistence in telling Schindler's story: "Schindler gave me my life, and I tried to give him immortality."[6]

accounts. Then they took goods by demanding that all Jewish property, including personal belongings, be registered. This made it easy for soldiers, SS officers, or any Aryan to simply raid Jewish homes and shops, taking whatever they wanted. No one stopped them. As one who lived through that time recalled, "They knocked on your door and four or five of them walked in and upset the whole apartment looking for valuables—furs and other things—and beating up people."[7]

The Nazis even took Jewish labor. The Forced Labor Decree of October 26, 1939, required that all Jews fourteen to sixty years of age work for a minimum of two years for Germans. That meant they could be snatched off the streets or dragged from their homes and forced to do whatever a German wanted. They were made to clear the streets of the rubble resulting from the German invasion. One man who served on many of these street-clearing crews recalled: "The army came in and took over parks, hotels, the school buildings, and they made a mess of them. They caught up people in the street to clean it up."[8]

Of all the policies imposed on the Jews by the General Government, however, the one that made Schindler rich was the Aryanizing, or Germanizing, of all businesses. Companies owned by Jews became the property of the Reich. A new government department, the East Trust Agency, assigned each business to a German trustee, or *Treuhänder*. The Jews who once owned the companies were required to become employees of the new owners. This ensured that the plant would continue operating, producing goods for the Fatherland. As soon as was practical, the Treuhänder was to fire Jewish workers and replace them with Aryans.

However, there were not enough Aryans in eastern Poland to take the place of the thousands of Jewish workers. And

A member of the German police kicks a Jew who is climbing onto the back of a truck during a roundup of forced labor. Two other Germans look on.

Germany needed the goods the Polish firms produced. So, for a while at least, Frank needed the Jews. But he did not have to pay them much for their services. He figured they should be grateful for the privilege of being allowed to stay alive.

Thus Krakow at the end of 1939 was a frightening hell to its sixty thousand Jews but a financial paradise to any German. Thriving businesses were being handed out to people with Aryan blood. Polish and Jewish laborers were available at ridiculously low wages. The army was clamoring for the manufacture of weapons, uniforms, and all kinds of supplies. This was a gold mine for an opportunist. And Oskar Schindler was an opportunist.

4

The Industrialist

Every opportunity in Poland for Germans came at the expense of Poland's Jews. Businesses and houses were available because they had been taken from Jews. Labor was cheap because Jews were not allowed to have money. German officials did not have to pay to have their apartments or streets cleaned because they could collar any Jew and demand the work be done. Even the amount of food that could be had was at the expense of Jews. Food was rationed during the war, and a Jew's ration was half that of a Pole, which was half that of a German.

The gross and obvious injustices done to Poland's Jews in the last months of 1939 were but a shadow of monstrous things to come. Hitler had made clear years earlier in his book *Mein Kampf* that he wanted to rid the world of Jews. Heydrich alluded in September 1939 to a "final aim," a secret solution to the "Jewish Question in the Occupied

Territory."[1] Hans Frank, governor of occupied Poland, wrote of the Jews in his diary: "We shall have to take steps . . . to extirpate [completely annihilate] them in some way—and this will be done."[2]

One of the first steps Frank took was to transport Jews from the countryside to a few large cities. This he did at the direction of Reinhard Heydrich. Heydrich knew that the concentration of his prey would make them easy to control while they were needed and easy to destroy when their usefulness was ended. The influx of rural Jews and the confiscation of property forced all Jews in these cities to cram together into just a few streets that would become ghettos.

The Nazis had an insidious way of maintaining order among their captive people. In each city they established a *Judenrat*, a council of Jewish leaders. These men were responsible for keeping track of the Jewish residents of the community, collecting any taxes or fees the occupiers decided to levy, selecting and delivering workers for the German-owned factories, and distributing the meager portions of food that were allotted. In short, they performed the dirty work of the day-to-day administration of Nazi injustice.

The Enamelware Factory

Schindler chose to bypass the *Judenrat* as he set about building his fortune. He knew its members had no real power. He always worked with people of genuine influence. When he learned of a factory he might be able to purchase, he sought out someone who had real connections to Jewish talent and money. He found that person in Itzhak Stern.

Stern had religious, political, economic, and social connections. As a scholar of Jewish literature, he had written articles that were published in religious journals. Politically he was a member of the Zionist Central Committee, an organization dedicated to the creation of a Jewish state in Palestine. He was vice president of the Jewish Agency for Western Poland. For the past fifteen years he had worked as the head of the accounting department of a large import-export firm in Krakow. He was well connected in the city's business community: he knew someone, often a relative or a friend, in nearly every factory.

Schindler was introduced to Stern by an old friend who had been made Treuhänder of the import-export company for which the accountant worked. Schindler also was Treuhänder, or trustee of a plant that had been seized from its Jewish owner. Now, however, he was considering leasing a business from the Court of Commercial Claims. Because of his experience in his father's farm machinery factory, he was interested in making machines or other metal products. A company called Rekord was available. It had gone bankrupt. It had been an enamelware factory, producing pots and pans, but sat empty for several years. Schindler asked Stern if he thought the business could be profitable again.

The accountant did not trust this smooth talking, confident German. "I was intensely suspicious of Schindler for a long time," he remembered later. "I suffered greatly under the Nazis. . . . I was very embittered."[3] But he told him the truth. With the cheap labor the new laws were offering German businessmen, the plant could easily turn out plenty of enamel kitchenware. The widening war meant that a great number of mess kits would soon be needed for the soldiers of the Reich. As for purchasing the equipment that would be needed to get the factory back into production, there might be Jews willing to invest. There were some who had not kept all their cash in banks.

One such Jew was Abraham Bankier. Bankier had been the manager of Rekord, and Schindler wanted to keep him in that position. Bankier introduced Schindler to men who had money but could not spend it. Jews were not allowed to have cash. What these once-wealthy men needed instead of currency were material goods. They needed items they could trade with willing Poles for food. They were happy to give Oskar Schindler their secret funds in exchange for the promise of metal pans.

So Schindler acquired a broken-down factory, a Jewish manager, and the materials he needed to begin operation. He renamed the enterprise Deutsche Emailwaren Fabrik, German Enamelware Factory. Most people knew it by its abbreviated name: Emalia. It was situated in Zablocie, a suburb of Krakow across the Vistula River. It began production in the winter of 1939–1940 with one hundred workers. Only seven of them were Jewish.

The First *Aktion*

While Schindler spent his days preparing to open his business, he used his evenings for schmoozing with the local bigwigs. He would treat them to extravagant dinners at the finest restaurants or cozy meals at his apartment. Emilie Schindler would host if she was in town. She did not move to Krakow until the spring of 1941. Schindler's parties always ended with more drinks than any of his guests could reasonably consume and more talk than they should have known was wise.

Among the authorities Schindler entertained were the leaders of the local SS police force and the SD Security Service. From them he learned some disturbing news. When the invasion of Poland was planned, Hitler had ordered that specially prepared SD squads would follow the army.

Their assignment was to terrorize, arrest, and murder the nobles, the intelligentsia (highly educated people), and the religious leaders of the conquered land. Some generals in the army protested the killing of civilians. They complained so strongly that Hitler agreed to delay the actions until the soldiers left. By the beginning of December 1940, the army was finished in Krakow. It was now the turn of the *Einsatzgruppen*, or action groups.

The Nazis always invented innocent-sounding terms for their most barbaric deeds. The expulsion of Jews from their ancient homes was called resettlement. The slaughter of leaders was a pacification action. There were no raids or killings; there were only actions, cleansings, special treatment, and executive measures. The first *Aktion* in Krakow was dubbed by SD Chief Heydrich as housecleaning.

From his drinking companions Schindler learned that this *Aktion* would be a coordinated raid on Jewish homes, businesses, and sacred places such as synagogues and cemeteries. By December, just three months since Poland came under the flag of the Reich, the authorities had completed the compulsory registration of all property belonging to Jews. This made the attack easy. The strategy was for SS thugs to bludgeon their way through the city, drag people into the streets, demand furs and jewelry, and take whatever they wished. At the same time the SD would head to the synagogues with axes, torches, and a lust for destruction and violence.

When Schindler heard of the plan, he knew the threat was real. He had seen Nazi terror in the Sudetenland. Although he could not guess how brutal the savagery would become, he had no doubt something horrible would take place. He could not stop it, but if he could warn people, perhaps it would not

Oskar Schindler (left) at a dinner party in Krakow. At parties like this, Schindler made contact with various SS and German officials, which often led to tips about impending deportations that enabled him to save his laborers.

be so bad for them. He would tell the most influential Jew he knew. It was only a small risk.

On the evening of December 3 Schindler went to Stern's apartment. They chatted as though they were friends, this well-to-do German and this Jew who had lost everything. They talked about books they had read, about the great authors. Stern served tea. Then, rather suddenly, almost as though it were an afterthought, Schindler spoke quietly, matter-of-factly. His words stunned the accountant: "I hear that there will be a raid on all remaining Jewish property tomorrow."[4]

Although still deeply mistrustful of Schindler, Stern decided he had nothing to lose in believing him. So he spread the word. Some who heard it packed their valuables and fled to the countryside for the next day or two. Those who did not were robbed and beaten. Some were caged in synagogues, forced to witness the desecration of all they held dear, and then shot while the synagogues burned.

Oskar Schindler's warning had proven to be true. In the first Nazi *Aktion* in Krakow, he had taken his first action to save Jews. It had been small; it had been easy. Just a few words over tea. Now it was time to get back to the business of making money.

The Business of War

War could be good business for a person with the right connections. Schindler certainly had connections everywhere. He had carefully cultivated relationships with officers in Hitler's army. He had worked his way up the ladder until he had close acquaintances on the board of the Armaments Inspectorate. This body was headed by General Julius Schindler, who was no relation. However, Oskar Schindler did not correct people when they assumed the two were

Hitler (right) rides in a car with Italian dictator Benito Mussolini. Germany, Italy, and Japan were the main Axis Powers of World War II. They battled the Allied Powers: United States, Great Britain, and the Soviet Union.

related. He used his name to suggest that the general would award him contracts to supply pots and pans to the army. If that did not work, he used bribes. For a bottle of vodka, an expensive watch, or a piece of furniture, one of his acquaintances in the Inspectorate would stamp his approval to Schindler's request for a government contract.

The items Schindler used for bribery were found by Poldek Pfefferberg. The young Jew could locate almost anything for Schindler on the streets of Krakow. He could also find outlets for the factory's goods. The city's black market not only supplied Schindler the means of getting what he wanted, but it also gave him customers for some of his wares.

Perhaps the most important connections Oskar Schindler had for his business were Abraham Bankier and Itzhak Stern. Bankier was a shrewd businessman; he ran the company. Stern became Emalia's accountant. Schindler was a salesman, a talker, a man who could close a deal. But he could not operate a factory. He was not disciplined enough to do mundane tasks. He did not know how to keep accounts. He could not keep from spending money. His strengths were winning contracts and finding other buyers. The rest he left to Bankier and Stern.

The two businessmen did an excellent job. By the end of 1940, in its first year of production, the Emalia factory had tripled in size. Schindler had managed to secure a contract for producing munitions as well as kitchenware. Emalia now employed three hundred workers. About half of these workers were Jewish.

Herr Direktor

The year 1940 was good for Schindler, but it was a growing nightmare for the Jews of the General Government. As more and more Jews displaced from Germany and western Poland poured in, their treatment became increasingly unbearable. Poles as well as Germans felt free to spit on, throw stones at, and otherwise terrorize Jews. Governor Hans Frank made it his goal to make at least his capital, Krakow, *Judenfrei*, free of Jews. He began the process in April, with a proclamation that all Jews must leave the city. A tiny fraction would be excepted: skilled workers needed for the war industries. This, of course, created a blitz of applicants at factories such as Emalia. The Schindler plant was an essential business, supplying equipment the soldiers could not do without. A Jew who worked there might be safe from the deportations that were sure to come.

The deportations, however, were not as fast or as thorough as Governor Frank would have liked. By March of 1941, eleven thousand Jews remained in Krakow. Until he could rid the city of these Jews, Frank would isolate them from the Aryan residents. The Nazi policy throughout Poland in 1940 and 1941 was to round up all Jews, bring them to a few large cities, and seal them off from the rest of the world. In the selected cities, thousands of victims were packed into ghettos that covered only a few blocks. The ghettos were surrounded by tall walls with barbed-wire fences on the top, armed police, and vicious dogs.

The Krakow Ghetto

Krakow's ghetto was established on March 3, 1941. It was in Podgorze, an area of the southern part of the city. In addition to the Jews who lived in Krakow, families from nearby cities and towns were brought in. The Jews who were imprisoned in Podgorze were forced to build their own fences. Portions of the enclosure were made from tombstones plundered from the city's Jewish cemetery. Within three weeks the walls were up and on March 20 the ghetto was closed. It occupied less than a tenth of a square mile: 656 by 437 yards. The sixteen blocks housed eighteen thousand people.[1]

All eighteen thousand were under the watchful eye of the Gestapo. The Gestapo had been placed in charge of the ghettos of Poland. This police agency ordered the *Judenrat* to appoint Jewish men to maintain order in the cramped enclave. The Jewish police force was called the *Ordnungsdienst* (OD). The Gestapo could control the thousands by controlling the few OD men. They exercised that control with the lash of a whip and the barrel of a gun.

Neither the Gestapo nor the OD, however, could control conditions inside the ghetto. With several people crammed into every room, the houses did not have adequate privacy,

50

Anna Duklauer Perl, *Sole Survivor of Her Family*

Before World War II, Anna Duklauer lived in the ski resort town of Zakopane in the mountains of Poland. With her father, mother, brother, and sister, she was forced into the Krakow ghetto when she was about twenty years old. Her mother and brother were killed in the ghetto. Anna, her father, and her sister were taken to Plaszow after the ghetto liquidation.

Working in the laundry room of the camp, Anna was beaten regularly. She went to work at Schindler's enamelware factory, first in Zablocie, then in Brinnlitz.

After liberation, Anna walked to Krakow and Zakopane looking for her family and friends. She learned that her mother and brother had perished in the death camps and all her friends had been shot. Her sister and three hundred others had been put in a boat that was purposely sunk. Her father had been poisoned days before liberation.

Without home or family, all she had to her name were a comb and a toothbrush. Eventually Anna married Jano Perl, another Holocaust survivor. They moved to Israel in 1965 and then to the United States. She died in March 1997.

Before the film *Schindler's List* revealed her story to the world, all Anna would say about that time was: "Without a man named Oskar Schindler, I wouldn't be here."[2]

Many Holocaust survivors lost several family members. These grave markers, bearing the Jewish star, were used for Jews killed by the Nazis.

heat, or water. The sewers overflowed. Diseases spread with deadly speed. Tempers flared and hope faded.

None of the squalor of the ghetto was of concern to Schindler. What was of interest to him was the change in the economic policy that resulted from the establishment of the ghettos. As long as the Jews were still in the city, the Nazis would use them to manufacture the goods Germany needed. They installed some factories inside the ghettos. For those plants outside the walls, the OD marched groups of workers to and from the sites. Once the ghetto was closed, Jews were not permitted to receive salaries for their work. Instead, their employers paid the SS and the worker received food rations instead of money. The cost for laborers was small, and the rations were barely enough to keep them alive. The Nazi policy amounted to slave labor.

For an industrialist such as Schindler, *Direktor* of a manufacturing plant, Jewish workers were far less expensive than Poles. As his company grew more successful, he looked to the ghetto to enlarge his workforce. Whenever he needed people, he simply told Abraham Bankier to arrange with the *Judenrat* for more Jews. For him, it was strictly a matter of good business.

Arrested

All of the good business Schindler enjoyed was not legal. He made money from his legitimate sales, but he also amassed a sizable fortune from selling to the black market. The German overseers of the General Government, of course, did not look kindly on such dealings. Any merchandise that reached the black market bypassed the control and taxes of the Nazi authorities. Either an informant told of Schindler's illegal transactions or someone saw his lavish spending and became suspicious of his growing wealth.

However the accusation came, the Gestapo paid Schindler a visit toward the end of 1941. The Gestapo seized all his account records and demanded that he accompany them to their headquarters. Schindler complied graciously; he was always gracious. He asked only for a moment so he could arrange to cancel his appointments for the day. Turning to Viktoria Klonowska, who had become his secretary, he scrawled a few names on a piece of paper. Then he smiled as he was led to the waiting car.

His secretary knew that Schindler had no appointments that day. She recognized the names on the list. One was a high-ranking *Abwehr* official; another was the chief of the SS police of Krakow. Two influential industrialists were also on the list. Each one was someone to whom Schindler had given generous gifts or who owed him a favor. It was time to collect.

By the next morning the Gestapo headquarters had received a number of telephone calls. Schindler was cleared of any wrongdoing and released. This would become a pattern: Oskar the adventurer would do as he wanted, risking serious consequences. Right at the brink of disaster, his charm and his money would save him.

His charm and his contacts, bought with his money, saved him when he was arrested again. This time Schindler's actions were far more innocent but his crime far more serious to the Nazi rulers. The incident occurred about six months after his first encounter with the Gestapo. The occasion was his thirty-fourth birthday, April 28, 1942.

The birthday was a cause for celebration at the enamelware factory. Schindler made every event a cause for celebration. He served cognac, one of his favorite drinks, to the people who worked in his offices. For the workers who operated the presses, lathes, and other equipment, he had white bread and

cigarettes, both luxuries in wartime Poland. The festivities were crowned with a magnificent cake. Schindler spared no expense; he could well afford to celebrate any way he wished. And he wished to share his merriment with all his employees.

The problem arose when groups of workers came from each section of the factory to bid their *Direktor* a happy birthday. In his normal exuberant style, perhaps made a little more enthusiastic by the liquor, Oskar thanked his employees. He shook hands heartily and hugged people energetically. He even kissed one young woman, and that was his mistake. For, whether or not Oskar knew it, the woman was Jewish. According to the laws of the Third Reich, for Germans to have such contact with Jews was treason.

The next morning the Gestapo came for Schindler. They did not take him to the hotel-like headquarters where they had questioned him before. Instead, they drove straight to Montelupich prison. Many people went into Montelupich but few came out. They had made the arrest in Emalia's yard without giving Schindler a chance to scribble any names. Still his secretary knew who to call. She also knew that another of Oskar's mistresses was connected with the *Abwehr*. The two of them managed to contact several of the friends Schindler had so carefully cultivated. After five days, he was let go with a stern reprimand. Again his charm and his money saved him.

The First Rescue

When charm and money would not work, Schindler used sheer bluster. That is how he effected the first rescue of some

**Men inside the Warsaw ghetto
try to smuggle in goods for their
fellow residents.**

of his employees. The issue that had placed them in need of rescue was the new identification card required of every resident of the ghetto.

The purpose of the new card was to separate those Jews who were of use to Germany from those who were not. The only reason Hitler had for keeping Jews alive was that some were needed for the war industries. So each was issued a *Kennkarte*, an identity card. For anyone employed in work deemed essential, a blue sticker, or *Blauschein*, was pasted on the card. The lines for the *Blauschein* were long, though some people did not realize how important the blue sticker was. They went about their business, planning to take care of the matter another day.

But for many, that day never came. One morning the SS swept through the ghetto. The officers had lists of names: names of people without stickers, people the Nazis did not need or want. With cold precision they called out the names one by one. Then they marched the long lines of those without a *Blauschein* to the railroad depot.

Among those whose names were on the list was Abraham Bankier, Schindler's right-hand man. Another employee had seen him standing near the trains and had reported it at the factory. Schindler could not afford to lose his office manager. So he drove to the depot.

What he found there stunned him. At least twenty cars lined the track. Some appeared to be already filled with Jews and several hundred people still stood in long rows. The very old

An elderly man and a child who have been rounded up for deportation wait with their luggage at an assembly point in the Krakow ghetto.

were there and the very young. Strong healthy men were there also, simply because they were in the wrong trade. No one had any baggage. They stood numbly, waiting for orders. The cars, labeled Resettlement Transports, were cattle cars. They had no beds, no seats, nothing at all of comfort. At that time, in the middle of 1942, no one in Krakow quite knew what happened to people who were going to be resettled in the east.

All Schindler knew was that he could not allow Bankier to leave. It was a matter of good business. He strode resolutely down the line of railroad cars, shouting for his office manager: "Bankier! Bankier! Bankier!" He complained loudly to an SS officer that his workers had been taken and he would not stand for it. Germany could not win the war if his factory could not manufacture the munitions the army needed. His employees were essential to the Reich and he wanted them right away.

The officer tried to argue, but he was no match for Schindler's swagger. The angry industrialist demanded the officer's name as though he, a civilian, somehow outranked him. He would report the officer's lack of cooperation. And he rattled off the names and titles of the authorities to whom he would make the report, obviously people he knew personally. He threatened to have the man sent to the fiercest battle lines at the Russian front.

The indignant bluff worked. The worried officer followed Schindler as he continued down the row of cars, calling for Bankier. Near the end, Bankier finally answered. Oskar commanded the frightened SS man to unbolt the door of the car. Along with the office manager, ten or twelve other Emalia workers spilled out.

Taking these Jews off a train, away from the SS, and out of the ghetto was risky business. A year earlier the head of the

General Government had issued a decree forbidding Jews to leave the ghetto without authorization. The punishment for disobeying the order was death. The decree also imposed a death sentence on any non-Jew who aided in defying the order:

> In accordance with . . . the Limitation of Residence in General Government . . . Jews leaving the Jewish Quarter without permission will incur the death penalty. According to this decree, those knowingly helping these Jews by providing shelter, supplying food, or selling them foodstuffs are also subject to the death penalty.[3]

Oskar Schindler was not in the habit of letting anything get in the way of what he wanted. He had broken other laws and escaped unscathed. He felt that keeping his business operating was more important than satisfying some ridiculous racial law.

As Schindler marched from the station with his dozen people, he left hundreds behind him in the windowless cattle cars. He left hundreds more standing beside the tracks. And thousands more were still in the ghetto, destined for the next wave of railroad cars. Neither Oskar Schindler nor the Jews in Krakow could imagine where and to what those cars were headed.

6

The Protector

The ghettos were never intended to be permanent. They merely served as a step in the resolution of what Hitler called the Jewish problem. From the very beginning, the Final Solution always meant the killing of Jews. The ghettos were simply holding pens. Jews were to be kept there and exploited until the Final Solution was practical.

After the ghetto, the next step was the establishment of labor camps. By the winter of 1941–1942, Germany desperately needed laborers. The *Blitzkrieg* (lightning-quick war) had begun to bog down. When Hitler invaded Russia in June 1941, he expected a rapid victory. Instead, the campaign dragged more soldiers into a long and bloody conflict. More Germans had to leave the factories of the homeland to fight in the army. That left German plants in need of workers.

The Reich's solution was to transform its concentration camps, which had been, at least officially, jails for political opponents and prisoners of war, into work camps. Though some of the camps had already used forced labor, the Nazis now made it official. During that deadly winter, the concentration camps held one hundred thousand inmates. They were put to work building roads, repairing bridges and railroad tracks, assembling bombs, and sewing uniforms.

At the same time the German war effort was searching for labor, some of Hitler's top men were meeting to discuss the Final Solution to what they considered the Jewish problem. When the Wannsee Conference ended in January 1942, both the labor problem and the Jewish question had been solved: "In big labor gangs . . . the Jews who are capable of work are brought to these areas (in the Eastern occupied territories) and employed in road building, in which task undoubtedly a large part will fall out through natural diminution [that is, death]."[1] The Jews would be brought to the camps and worked to death. The chief inspector of the concentration camps was told to expect one hundred thousand Jewish men and fifty thousand Jewish women within thirty days.

The influx of so many meant that new camps would need to be built. Others would have to be enlarged. Auschwitz, which was opened in 1940 as a prison camp, became the biggest. When it was changed to a slave-labor camp, four hundred different companies relocated to the massive compound of camps and subcamps. It was located just forty miles from Krakow.

Just as the ghetto was only a step toward the Final Solution, the labor camp was also just another stage. The ultimate solution was the extermination camp. From the very start the plan had been wholesale murder. Hitler had proclaimed on several occasions that the result of his war would be "the annihilation of the Jewish race throughout Europe."[2]

Even more quickly than the prison camps had been turned into slave-labor camps, some of the slave-labor camps became annihilation centers. New killing sites opened as well. Before 1942 ended, six extermination camps were in operation: Chelmno, Belzec, Sobibór, Treblinka, Majdanek, and Auschwitz. All were in Poland.

The hundreds of other camps were actually killing facilities as well. They did not have gas chambers where mass murder was obvious and deliberate. They killed their inmates through less direct means: impossibly hard labor, disease-ridden quarters, starvation rations, shootings, hangings, and undisguised brutality.

At the Wannsee Conference the responsibility for carrying out the Final Solution had been entrusted to SD Security Chief Reinhard Heydrich. He called it "Operation Reinhard." It was a diabolically simple plan. All Jews who were not murdered outright were to be isolated in ghettos where harsh conditions would kill the weakest. The ones who survived would be sent to labor camps where rigorous work would kill most. The ghettos and labor camps would gradually be emptied, or liquidated, through one *Aktion* after another. Anyone left would be taken to the death camps where poison gas would kill them all.

June *Aktion*

The first *Aktion* in the Krakow ghetto occurred from May 28 to June 8, 1942. To give it the appearance of a reasoned operation, people with a *Blauschein* were separated from those without. It made some sense, however twisted. Those whose jobs were essential to Germany would stay; others would be taken somewhere else. Exactly where they were going no one knew. And what would happen to them there no one could imagine. Rumors had begun to drift into the ghetto, but they were too horrid to be believed.

However logical the raids may have seemed, the scope and suddenness stunned the already frightened Jews. Gestapo and SS police descended on the sleeping ghetto, rousting people from their beds and pushing them into the streets. Everyone was told to assemble at Plac Zgody, the central yard of the Jewish sector. The name, ironically, meant Peace Square. There they were divided into two lines: those who were of economic use to the Reich and those who were not. The sheer cruelty of the operation was incomprehensible. One victim described the scene:

> The soldiers were running all over our house and all over the building, chasing people out, asking for their IDs and just shoving people out the door. . . . It was a feeling of absolute fear. . . . People who couldn't make it, who carried bundles that were too heavy, were just simply shot.[3]

Those who tried fruitlessly to hold onto their meager possessions were not the only ones shot. Anyone who resisted, in even the smallest way, was killed without ceremony or mercy. The chairman of the *Judenrat* defied orders and was slain. The police made a second sweep of the residences. People who were found trying to hide were thrown to the street and executed on the spot. When the *Aktion* was over, three hundred people were dead on the streets and six thousand were removed from the ghetto. They were taken by cattle car to eastern Poland, to the Belzec extermination camp.

The SS may have thought the only witnesses to the mass murder of so many of Krakow's citizens were their fellow Jews. That did not bother the killers because those witnesses would be victims of the next *Aktion*. However, the SS was wrong. There was another witness.

On one of the June mornings, Oskar Schindler had decided to go horseback riding. He had horses that he had purchased from a Polish countess who needed money. With his mistress Amelia, he rode through the wooded hills overlooking the ghetto. At first the scene below them may have seemed a simple curiosity, one of the many Nazi attempts to organize and control a conquered people. But as the shouted commands of the police and the barking of the Dobermans gave way to the sounds of tortured screams and gunshots, Schindler sat frozen on his horse. This was worse than he had seen in Czechoslovakia. This went beyond the sadistic celebration that had occurred when the German army first entered Krakow. This was the vicious slaughter of an entire group of people. "Beyond this day," Schindler declared later, "no thinking person could fail to see what would happen. I was now resolved to do everything in my power to defeat the system."[4]

Sanctuary

Oskar Schindler's first deliberate act against the system was to build a place of refuge for his Jewish employees. If they did not have to return to the ghetto at night, they would not have to face the whips, clubs, and pistols in the morning. Shortly after the June *Aktion*, Schindler was able to buy the factory he had leased along with the empty land around it. The property now belonged to him and he could build whatever he wished on it.

As with most of Schindler's ventures, the addition to his property began with one of the contacts he had cultivated. Not far from Emalia stood a plant that manufactured wooden boxes. The original owner, Szymon Jereth, was managing the operation under a German *Treuhänder*. One never knew when lumber might come in handy, so Schindler had made friends with Jereth and the *Treuhänder*. From Jereth, Schindler obtained enough lumber to build a simple shelter. Jereth's only stipulation was that the crude structure could be a refuge for employees of the box factory if necessary.

The shelter became increasingly necessary. Whenever Schindler learned of upcoming trouble in the ghetto, he kept his night-shift workers—along with Jereth's—at his factory overnight. When the OD men came to march them back to their crowded tenements, Schindler invented an excuse as to why he needed them to stay with him. It was one way to defeat the system.

Even before the shelter was built, the Emalia factory had a reputation as something of a sanctuary. The work was hard, but no one was beaten or even hit. The food was a little more substantial than in the other factories. The German who owned the business was good. One of the first Jewish women to be employed there recalled what it was like:

> I started to go to the [ghetto] employment office for work. Every day, Germans used to come and pick girls to work. A man [Abraham Bankier] came in and looked us over. He chose six of us: "You are going with me to work. . . . " We didn't know what we were doing there. Then I saw a tall, handsome, gorgeous man—I really was struck by how beautiful he was. I saw a good face, smiling at us. I was not scared. He said, "Children, don't worry. Who works for me, lives through the war."[5]

Those who worked for Schindler lived through the brutal *Aktion* of October 27–28, 1942. If the thinning of the ghetto in June seemed to follow some sort of logic, all reason was lost by October. In the summer, residents with blue stickers had been spared. By fall, no excuse was given for who would be shipped to the death camps now and who would go later. The head of the *Kommissariat*, which had replaced the *Judenrat*, was told to prepare a list of four thousand residents who would be relocated. When he refused, the SS swept down on Podgorze again, disregarding the *Blauschein* and tearing to pieces any *Arbeitsbescheinigung*, or permit to work for the German military. They completely destroyed the ghetto hospital, orphanage, and home for the aged, along with everyone in them. At the end of this *Aktion*, six hundred lay dead and seven thousand ended up in the transports. Most were shipped to Belzec and some were taken to Auschwitz. In February, Auschwitz had been designated an Operation Reinhard extermination camp. None of Emalia's workers were among those killed or taken in the cattle cars. They had spent the night and morning of the *Aktion* in the plain wooden sanctuary at the enamelware factory.

Mission to the Outside World

Oskar Schindler's reputation as a man sympathetic to the miseries of the Jews spread among Jews beyond the ghetto. His name was known in Istanbul, Turkey and Budapest, Hungary among groups of Jewish activists. The activists belonged to a network of Zionist organizations, the Zionists working to establish a homeland for Jews in Palestine. Schindler's accountant, Itzhak Stern, belonged to the Zionist Central Committee and was vice president of the Jewish Agency for Western Poland. His brother Nathan and at least two other Emalia workers were also connected with the underground Zionist movement.

The Zionist organizations communicated regularly with one another. However, once Hitler took over huge chunks of Europe, the Zionists living under the flag of the swastika fell silent. Those outside the rapidly enlarging German realm sent secret delegations into Nazi-held territories in an attempt to discover the situation there. The man dispatched to Krakow was an Austrian dentist named Sedlacek. He came from Budapest with a list of names of people who might know what was happening to Poland's Jews and, more importantly, might care. Oskar Schindler's name was on that list.

Schindler was at first reluctant to tell the dentist what he knew. He was not afraid of betraying his party. He was concerned that no one would believe him. People outside the Third Reich might believe that Jews were being harassed and even badly mistreated, but who would believe they were being slaughtered, that the entire people was being intentionally obliterated? Who would imagine that a nation at war would dedicate so much of its weaponry, its transportation facilities, and its human and material resources to a cause with no military or economic benefit?

As Dr. Sedlacek listened, he recognized that this German saw the situation as few other people could. He saw it from the perspective of the SS officers he drank with. Schindler understood the chiefs of the wartime agencies, who considered Jews nothing more than expendable cogs in the military production machine. He saw through the eyes of his employees; men and women who trudged to work under armed guard with empty stomachs, broken bodies, and crushed hearts.

Schindler's own view, that of an observer rather than a participant or a victim, was one of outrage. He reported objectively and clearly. Years later, in 1964, he recalled what he told the Austrian dentist and why:

> The persecution of Jews in the General Government in Polish territory gradually worsened in its cruelty. In 1939 and 1940 they were forced to wear the Star of David and were herded together and confined in ghettos.

67

> In 1941 and 1942 this unadulterated sadism was fully
> revealed. And then a thinking man, who had overcome
> his inner cowardice, simply had to help. There was no
> other choice.[6]

Schindler was in the process of overcoming his inner cowardice. He had to help. One way of helping was to give the dentist an accurate picture of life for Jews under Nazism. Dr. Sedlacek was stunned. He had cash stuffed in the false bottom of his suitcase. The Zionists in Budapest had obtained the money from the American Joint Distribution Committee, a welfare organization. They had hoped it would relieve whatever hardships Poland's Jews were suffering. But they had no idea of the enormity of the persecution. No amount of money could fix this. No small Zionist group could rescue the Jews of Europe. The world needed to know.

The dentist asked Schindler to go to Budapest and make a report to his superiors. Perhaps they could convince England or the United States to help. Despite the dangers of being discovered with Jewish sympathizers, Schindler went. But the Zionists in Hungary found his story just as he had feared they would: unbelievable. They dismissed his testimony as an exaggeration of the struggles Jews had endured for centuries. Schindler returned to Krakow, alone in his determination to defeat the system and keep as many Jews as he could from being destroyed.

Plaszow

Part of Schindler's report described a camp in the village of Plaszow on the outskirts of Krakow. The camp was part of a new Nazi military strategy. As the war dragged on and the ranks of the Reich's armies grew thinner, young Germans left their factory jobs to become soldiers. This created a desperate need for new workers. The concentration camps, which then held political prisoners, were ready-made labor pools. German efficiency turned them into forced-labor camps. And Nazi anti-Semitism filled them with Jews. Hundreds of new camps were created to supply the German war machine and produce goods for the homeland.

About the time of the summer *Aktion* in Podgorze, the SS had decided to turn the village of Plaszow into one of those labor camps. They evicted the residents from their homes and built the camp on top of two Jewish cemeteries. People from the ghetto were put to work uprooting the tombstones and erecting buildings on the graves of their parents and grandparents. They constructed barracks for the men and women who would be brought here to live and work. They built factories where they would produce goods for their enemies. They broke up the headstones and used them to make the camp's roads. They surrounded the compound with two and a half miles of electrified barbed-wire fence.

The camp was completed in December 1942. As soon as the drafty buildings were finished, Jews from the ghetto were moved into them. One of the first to arrive described the scene: "It was bad. There were barracks with wooden platforms: a lower level, middle level, and upper level. . . . We could take only what we could carry with us. A platform filled with straw was what you slept on."[7]

The camp factories supported the German war effort. Some made uniforms for the soldiers at the front. Some repaired the vehicles of the military staff. Others manufactured tools, paper, envelopes, and brushes. The camp commanders turned everything to profit. A survivor recalled, "We used to dig up the old graves, dig out the bodies, and take out the teeth. They gave us tools. You pull them out with pliers: just the gold."[8]

By March 1943 Plaszow had two thousands residents. The ghetto had thousands more. That was to change with the arrival of the new camp commandant, Amon Goeth.

Liquidation of the Ghetto

Goeth came to Krakow with orders to liquidate its ghetto. In the vocabulary of the Third Reich, liquidate meant clear out, demolish, remove all trace of, completely obliterate. Goeth had the honor of completing the task of making Krakow *Juderein*, cleansed of Jews. He had already wiped out ghettos in other cities, so he was prepared.

Krakow, also, was prepared. After the October *Aktion*, the tiny Jewish sector was divided in two to make liquidation easier. Section A housed the workers, those who were still of some use to their oppressors. The rest lived in Section B. Goeth would first clear Section A, taking everyone to Plaszow. Emptying Section B would then be very simple.

Goeth chose March 13, a Jewish sabbath, to begin the liquidation. He arrived early, before the first light, at Plac Zgody, the central square of the ghetto. With him were men of the *Sonderkommando*, the special unit formed for just such brutal jobs as this. It began much like every other Aktion, with ferocious shouts, vicious shoves, snarling dogs, and the sounds of gunfire. But there was a sharper fury to this operation—a finality. Once the residents who survived the violence of the Aktion were herded from Podgorze toward Plaszow, the Sonderkommando went through Section A a second time. They tore walls apart, ripped up floors, fired their weapons through attics. The hundreds of people who

Portrait of Amon Goeth while in Polish custody as an accused war criminal.

70

were found hiding were slaughtered on the spot. Their bodies were carted to Plaszow and thrown into two mass graves at the edge of the camp.

The next day the scene was repeated in Section B. The only difference was that no one from this section went to the forced-labor barracks. Instead, they were loaded into cattle cars and taken to the extermination camps of Belzec and Auschwitz.

Schindler's employees were spared the horrors of those two days in March. His acquaintances among the Gestapo and the SS had been excited about taking part in the historic event, so Schindler knew something of what was to come and when. One of his workers explained how he protected them:

> He went around the factory and talked to everybody in groups, or individually. He told us we couldn't go back in the ghetto because there was an *Aktion*. I don't remember him using the word [for] liquidation, but *Aktion*, that the Jews were being shipped out or whatever. That scared me horribly, to a point where I was actually unable to eat.[9]

But Schindler could not keep his Jews, the *Schindlerjuden*, at Emalia for long. After a few days, Goeth required that they all be housed in Plaszow.

Life in Plaszow

Every injustice, every atrocity made Oskar Schindler all the more determined to beat the system, to cheat the Nazis out of another victim. Besides, he was getting to know some of the Jews he was harboring. At first he spoke mainly with Stern, Bankier, and the few others who worked in the office. But as they gradually brought others into the factory, he came to know those on the floor too. Some had been with him more than three years. He called them all his children.

Leon Leyson, *Teenager*

Born September 15, 1929, Leon was thirteen when the Krakow ghetto was liquidated. With one brother, he worked at a brush and broom factory in the ghetto while his father and another brother worked at Emalia. He survived the Krakow ghetto liquidation by hiding in the crawlspace of a shed. After the liquidation, he was taken to Plaszow and his arm tattooed with the mark of the concentration camp. The teenager sucked out as much ink as he could so that only a thin line remained.

Leon learned to be a machinist by working alongside his father at Emalia and Brinnlitz. He was so small he had to stand on a box to reach the handles of the machines at the Brinnlitz factory. Schindler called him "Little Leyson."

Many Holocaust survivors' homes had been destroyed or taken over. As a result, they had to live in displaced persons camps.

After liberation, the family spent time in a displaced persons camp in Germany. Two brothers had died early in the war. The remaining brother and sister went to Israel, and Leon went with his parents to the United States. He was drafted into the U.S. Army in 1951 and served in the Korean War. He completed his education in California, studying the machinist trade. From 1958 to 1995, he taught shop at Huntington Park High School in Los Angeles.[10]

Leon Leyson met Schindler for the first time after the war in 1972. Schindler recognized him after twenty-seven years and called him by name.

"I knew the people who worked for me," he once said. "When you know people, you have to behave toward them like human beings."[11]

Treating his Jews like human beings meant helping them survive the hellhole that was Plaszow. There the food rations were even smaller than in the ghetto. Any families that were still intact were split, men going to one set of barracks and women to another. In the ghetto, movement had been restricted; in the camp, every second was strictly controlled. In Podgorze, torture and death could come any time; in Plaszow, they were present every hour.

Amon Goeth ran the camp with a chilling sadism. Emilie Schindler called him "the most despicable man I have ever met in my whole life."[12] He carried a revolver at all times and kept two Great Danes that were trained to tear human flesh. If one prisoner escaped, he had twenty-five shot. If one was found with an extra potato, his entire barracks would be stripped and flogged. He killed people for speaking, for smiling, for not shining his shoes properly. Goeth shot down camp inmates like tin cans on a fence. He needed no reason. As lord of Plaszow, he answered to no one—at least to no one who would disagree with his indiscriminate murders. He "couldn't have breakfast or lunch without seeing Jewish blood," one prisoner said. "Every day, he would shoot somebody else at random, hunting like an animal in the jungle. . . . He would come to the barracks and wouldn't leave till he shot a few people."[13]

Schindler heard what life was like in Plaszow from his employees. But hearing about the atrocities did not prepare him for actually seeing them. He observed the horrors firsthand when Itzhak Stern failed to show up for work. The accountant had become very sick and his friends who marched every day to Emalia begged Schindler to go to the camp to help him. He went several times, bringing medicine that kept Stern alive.

On one of those occasions, he saw all the women being summoned to the *Appellplatz*, the large square where roll call was held every morning and evening. Two of their number who had tried to run away from the camp had been captured. For this crime, they were being hanged. The rest were being forced to stand in the common area and witness the executions. One of the prisoners described the event and Schindler's reaction: "All women [were ordered] to *Appell* [role call] for hanging. Schindler came and saw Goeth shoot them two seconds before they died hanging. Schindler vomited in front of everybody. He would never be working for the Germans again, he said."[14]

Already he had determined, while watching the June 1942 *Aktion* in Krakow, that he would do everything he could to defeat the Nazi system. Although he continued to wear the swastika on his lapel, he had already resolved he would work against the Germans:

> I was a Nazi, and I believed that the Germans were doing wrong . . . when they started killing innocent people. And it didn't mean anything to me that they were Jewish, to me they were just human beings. . . . I decided I'm going to work against them [the Nazis] and I'm going to save as many as I can.[15]

But after witnessing the senseless Nazi brutality at such close range, his resolve became passionate. From this point on, according to Stern, Schindler became fanatical in his determination to defeat the Nazi system and to save as many Jews as he could. No longer would he be a war profiteer who simply treated his employees, some of whom happened to be Jewish, better than other industrialists. He would defy the

Henry Rosner, *Camp Musician*

Born March 2, 1905, in Krakow, Henry Rosner was the oldest of nine children. Before the war, the five Rosner brothers had a band that was popular in Krakow.

At Plaszow, Henry played violin, his brother Poldek played the accordion, and his brother William played the bugle. Henry and Poldek entertained at many of Amon Goeth's

This prisoner band performs at Auschwitz concentration camp.

parties. They played when the commandant had a hard time sleeping. Goeth loved music. Because of their positions as Goeth's musicians, they received favored treatment and escaped many of the atrocities of Plaszow.

At Gröss-Rosen, on the way to Brinnlitz, Henry's violin was taken from him. Schindler went to the camp and brought it back. He gave it to Henry's wife, saying, "It is the same instrument, only a different tune."

With his son Olek, Henry was in a group of fathers and sons taken in Schindler's absence from Brinnlitz to Auschwitz. From there they were sent to the camp at Dachau.

Immediately after the war, Henry and his wife Manci provided housing in Munich for the Schindlers. In 1946, the Rosens emigrated to the United States. Henry made his living playing his violin in New York City's restaurants and hotels. He died December 3, 1995.[16]

hateful, bloodthirsty designs of his party's leaders. He would not merely take in and protect a few friends and relatives of his workers. He would open all of his resources to all the Jews he could:

> He stopped worrying about the production of enamel-ware appliances for *Wehrmacht* [German armed forces] barracks and began the conspiring, the string-pulling, the bribery, and the shrewd outguessing of Nazi officialdom that finally were to save so many lives. . . . For the next two years, Oskar Schindler's ever-present obsession was how to save the greatest number of Jews.[17]

Saving Jews was not the same as simply protecting them. It would require more than warning a leader of an upcoming *Aktion*, rescuing a few workers from a transport, sheltering some overnight in his factory. Saving Jews would take bold ideas and bold action. If anyone could do it, Schindler could. He was a man of boldness.

7

The Labor Camp Operator

When Schindler's workers went to Plaszow, in the spring of 1943, Germany was losing the war. Its armies in the east were bogged down in the frozen ground of the Soviet Union. In the west, Great Britain was refusing to surrender. The United States had entered the conflict: German forces were stretched thin. But as Hitler's war against Europe was slowing down, his war against the Jews was ratcheting up.

The world war was the ideal camouflage for the Final Solution. While the eyes of the nations were on the open battlefields, Hitler was pursuing his secret war in hidden gas chambers. While presidents and generals focused on troops, Hitler was massacring civilians. Newspapers reported battle casualties but ignored accounts of mass murders of women and children—reports from sources like Schindler and Sedlacek. So barbaric men such as Amon Goeth continued to degrade and torture Jews in forced-labor camps.

Schindler had determined to save as many as he could from people like Goeth. He had about four hundred Jews in his employ. They were marched every day under armed guard to and from their new quarters in Plaszow, three miles away. His first step in saving them was to ensure that Plaszow would not be liquidated as the ghetto and other camps had been. The camp, actually a very small contributor to the Nazi economy, had to be seen as indispensable.

Schindler took care of that easily. He called on one of the friends he had made upon his arrival in Krakow four years earlier. General Schindler, chief of the Armaments Inspectorate, awarded contracts for the manufacture of goods for the military. Schindler had earlier talked him into allowing the Emalia factory to produce the V–2 rockets that Hitler hoped would crush his enemies. Now, over a bottle of vodka, Schindler convinced the general that the products Plaszow's factories could supply were necessary for German victory. Goeth's factories, as well as Emalia, began receiving more orders from the military.

The Schindler Subcamp

Schindler realized, however, that simply giving his Jews employment in an essential industry did not guarantee their survival. They could be gunned down by Goeth or attacked by his dogs without any provocation. As long as they lived at Plaszow they were not safe. The only way he could protect them was to keep them with him at Emalia. To do that, he offered to turn his factory into a subcamp of Plaszow.

A subcamp in Zablocie would help the war effort, he argued to the officials who made such decisions. The workers would be closer to their jobs. He would build the camp, the barracks, guard houses, watch towers, and nine-foot fences, at his own expense. The costs of installing a kitchen, laundry,

Commandant Amon Goeth delivers a speech to the SS staff in the Plaszow concentration camp.

bathhouse, latrines, and all the other requirements for a forced-labor camp would come out of his profits. He would even be willing to house workers for nearby factories that made boxes and radiators. Most of the other industrialists had moved their operations into Plaszow, taking advantage of Goeth's offer of free space and laborers. Schindler was proposing to pay all his expenses. Since there were other ghettos still to be liquidated, other Jews to be brought to Plaszow, Schindler's request was granted. Thus Schindler the industrialist became Schindler the labor camp operator. The only way he could defeat the system, as he had vowed to do after the 1942 *Aktion*, was to become part of it.

Schindler's camp, however, was far different from Goeth's. At Emalia there were no beatings, no humiliations, no killings. The daily rations at Plaszow amounted to 700–1,100 calories; Schindler smuggled in enough black market food to supply his workers with 2,000 calories. In the factories of Plaszow, inmates worked fourteen- and eighteen-hour days; at Emalia they worked twelve. Unlike Plaszow, Emalia workers had soap and hot water.

Goeth's men looked for ways to make the tortured lives of their prisoners even more miserable. They made the emaciated members of work crews carry large rocks to and from their assignments just to see them bowed under the heavy burdens. Schindler, on the other hand, found ways of making life in a Nazi labor camp more bearable for his Jews. By bribing the camp's guards he was able to provide medicine. For the many who liked to smoke, he would light a cigarette, take a puff or two, and throw it on the factory floor. Sometimes he would set down and forget a nearly full pack of cigarettes on an office employee's desk. He celebrated his birthday, his anniversary, and any other occasion he could think of with extra bread for everyone.

The SS guards were not permitted on the factory floor except during mandatory inspections. Schindler even tried to protect his people during the required inspections. He had a switch installed in his office that would ring a bell at the workstations. The bell warned his employees whenever an inspector was in the compound. One grateful survivor compared Goeth's camp and Schindler's subcamp:

> Emalia was entirely different circumstances [from Plaszow]. Schindler was always kind. He was never screaming on anybody. . . . Usually when the SS came for inspection, Schindler wined them and dined them and later took them for inspection, but they never bothered to hit anybody.[1]

Schindler gave his Jews more than work and food, more than mere existence. He gave them some enjoyment in their otherwise dreary lot. He set aside a portion of his property as a soccer field and found balls so they could play in the afternoons. He smuggled letters in and out of Krakow, so workers could communicate with their children who were being hidden by non-Jews. He refused to enforce strict segregation of men and women, allowing sweethearts and families to spend some time together.

Just as importantly, he gave them dignity. He treated them with common courtesies. He called them by name. He bowed to each of his employees when he greeted them. Sometimes he winked at the prettier ones. One survivor recalled:

> Us he treated with respect, like a gentleman. One of the worst effects on me was the way we were treated by the others, the lack of respect, the degradation. If they saw a Jewish woman they would kick her, beat her, would throw her onto the ground and shoot her. They treated us worse than dogs. And here comes a German,

who is the manager of a factory for whom you work, and he speaks to you like one human being to another, with a "please" and "thank you" and a smile. . . . "Everything will be all right, don't be afraid," [he'd say]. And the moment someone smiled and bent down to tell you all would be well, it was . . . like an angel speaking, like God had sent him to lift up our morale. And because of this high morale people didn't get sick or die.[2]

Despite Schindler's efforts to make Emalia a humane place, the factory in Zablocie was still a Nazi forced-labor camp. The workers were prisoners, the tasks were hard, and armed SS men stood in guard towers. But death did not stalk every station and every corridor. "By Schindler," one inmate explained, "we were hungry, but not starving. We were cold, but not freezing. We had fear, but we were not beaten."[3]

Enlarging the Subcamp

Part of Schindler's plan to defeat the system was to transfer as many Jews as he could from Plaszow to Emalia. When he built the subcamp, he included barracks for twelve hundred inmates. He did his best to fill those barracks. Whenever he could justify placing additional workers, he would send word to the officials at the camp that he needed ten, twenty, or thirty more prisoners.

People in Plaszow wanted to be in Schindler's subcamp; going there meant getting on the right list. Nazis were meticulous list makers. Life in the camps was controlled by the lists. There were lists of who went to the easier work details and who went to the hardest; who would stay under Amon Goeth's trigger-happy eye and who could work in the factories outside the camp; who would remain in the camp of the living and who would go to the death camps.

In their fiendish way of running things, the camp commanders had placed prisoners in charge of camp order. It was

Victor Dortheimer,
Goeth and Schindler's Painter

Victor Dortheimer was born on September 16, 1918, in Krakow, Poland. His father, Herman, was killed at Mauthausen when the camp hospital staff injected gasoline directly into his heart. His mother, Fransisca, was transported to the Belzec death camp in the summer 1942 *Aktion* and died there. His brother Michael joined the Polish army and was killed early in World War II. His brother David was executed by Amon Goeth with his entire labor detail because someone in the group had a small amount of food in his possession.

Victor painted and decorated Goeth's villa at Plaszow. When Schindler asked Goeth for some men to do some painting for him, Victor was in the group. The foreman, when asked the number of men in the party, was not sure, so Goeth shot him. Victor was deputy foreman. Before Goeth could ask him the same question, Schindler selected Victor for his painter and took him to Emalia. Victor once hit a Polish worker at Schindler's factory and confessed to Schindler before the worker could complain. Schindler replied, "Victor, don't worry, do it again if you have to."

After the war, Victor and his wife Helena had a son and moved to Israel. The marriage dissolved. Victor married again and moved to England. He died there on May 9, 2000.

Only four of the fifty Dortheimer relatives survived World War II and the Holocaust.[4]

their way of diverting the inmates' anger from their captors to their fellow Jews. Jewish block leaders were punished if the prisoners in their barracks did not report for roll call, were insolent, or broke any rule. And Jewish inmates drew up the lists.

Plaszow's list maker was Marcel Goldberg. The camp commanders always tried to find the harshest or most corruptible prisoners to exercise control over other inmates. Goldberg was such a person. Even before Plaszow, in the ghetto, he had a reputation as a cruel man without principles. Plaszow prisoners described him as "a wild animal,"[5] a "manhandler,"[6] "a bandit,"[7] someone who "should die before he was born."[8] As head of the labor office in the camp, lord of the lists, Goldberg was open to bribes.

Some of the prisoners had the means to offer bribes. They may not have had adequate food or decent shoes, but some had cash or jewelry. They had brought gold and diamonds from the ghetto, sewn in the lining of their clothes, taped to the bottoms of their feet, held under their tongues, drilled into their teeth. They had taken what they could, hoping they would still have it when the nightmare was over. Some gave their meager treasures to Goldberg in exchange for a spot on a good list.

Even when names were not on the right list, Schindler managed to get some people into Emalia. He too bought their way in with gifts. The prisoners bribed Goldberg; Schindler often bribed Goeth or other Plaszow officers. Dolek Horowitz asked Schindler to bring his wife and two children; they cost an envelope of jewelry. Regina Perlman, a Jewish girl who lived in Krakow as a Polish Aryan, pleaded with Schindler to take her parents out of Plaszow. He knew neither the girl nor her parents, but he found them and took them into his camp.

Ryszard (Richard) Horowitz,
Youngest Survivor

Born May 5, 1939, Ryszard Horowitz was only three years old when the Krakow ghetto was liquidated. He was barely six years old when World War II ended on May 8, 1945. He was probably the youngest of the *Schindlerjuden.*

Ryszard was sheltered with his family at both Emalia and Brinnlitz. Because of his age, he was taken with his father to Auschwitz. From there, his father was sent to Mauthausen. Ryszard was hidden by another Auschwitz inmate in a barracks used to quarantine people with typhus.

With other children who survived Auschwitz, he was taken after the war to an orphanage in Krakow. While leaving the camp, he appeared in a newsreel.

His mother and sister, freed from Brinnlitz, saw the news report, recognized Ryszard, and began searching for him. He had been taken in by a family friend.

After a few months, Ryszard was reunited with his mother and his sister. The whole family was reunited when his mother saw his father on a street in Krakow.

Ryszard Horowitz was educated at Krakow's Academy of Fine Arts. He emigrated to the United States in 1959. He became one of America's best commercial photographers.

When Horowitz's own children reached the age he was when Schindler saved him, he recalled the camps: "I still find it unbelievable that I was there."[9]

Itzhak Stern asked for the rabbi Menasha Levartov. Goeth had attempted to shoot him three times but each time the gun had misfired. Somehow Schindler got him in. He got thirty prisoners transferred from Plaszow to Emalia as part of the purchase of a car, a car that was reclaimed by Goeth's officer the very next day. The officer kept the car and Schindler kept the prisoners. Before long every bed in the camp was filled.

Outwitting the SS

Getting people into his factory was not enough to defeat the system. They had to be protected inside the factory. Emalia was a subcamp of Plaszow, so Schindler was technically under Goeth and his SS squads. He hosted and attended parties with Goeth and other important officials, keeping strong any contacts he might need. He kept them in his debt with black-market sausages and vodka. But the lower-level SS men, the ones who came for periodic inspections, were always looking for ways to discredit a wealthy industrialist. And they took every opportunity to humiliate and torture Jews.

Survivors tell many stories of times Schindler saved them from the SS. They recount the time he protected Sam Soldinger. Sam was in double jeopardy. First, he was young, barely sixteen. Emalia was a work camp, and no children were supposed to be on its premises. But Schindler tried to keep families together and he loved children. Very few children were in the camp. Only a miraculous few survived the deportations, the ghetto liquidation, and the searching eyes of the SS. On paper, no one in Schindler's employ was under age fifteen.

Sam, besides being young, had a headache. He had gone to Emalia's three-bed infirmary. The subcamp's doctor described what happened: "He was resting in a bunk, and suddenly one

87

of Goeth's people came to see the place with Schindler. They saw the [boy]: 'What is he doing here?' They wanted to kill him because he didn't look sick." But Oskar talked them out of it.[10]

Another child in danger was Leon Leyson. He was only fourteen and too small to work the lathes and drills of the enamelware factory. So Schindler stood him on a box so he could reach the handles of the machines. Then, in his boldness, Schindler boasted to the inspectors about him. Leon later described the situation:

> He used to point me out when he brought in his superiors, doing his PR to show how his company was really operating—how well they were doing, the Jews were working, and all that. I was never certain what he was going to do. I knew then that I should not be conspicuous, because I was a kid, so when he singled me out . . . I'd worry. . . . They would come up real close and watch me work. Now, *that* was really scary. He'd bring in huge, monstrous-looking SS with the skull and crossbones on their uniforms. They'd walk up and I'd be petrified. They would stand real close to me, on the other side of the machine. I wouldn't dare look up, so all I could see was these big belt buckles on the uniforms.[11]

By singling out Little Leyson for praise, Schindler made sure the SS did not harm him or any of the handful of other little people in his factory.

Then there is the story of the Wohlfeilers. All five worked at Emalia. The Gestapo uncovered forged documents with false Aryan identities made out to this family. Two agents came to the camp to arrest them. This time Schindler defeated the system with one of his favorite weapons: cognac. He later said of the incident: "Three hours after they walked in, two drunken Gestapo men reeled out of my office without their prisoners and without the incriminating documents they had demanded."[12]

Sometimes it was not the SS or the Gestapo that threatened the *Schindlerjuden*, but German and Polish workers who had jobs in the subcamp. A German foreman placed Rena Ferber in danger one day. She had been working in the ammunition section and had just been moved from a small machine to a giant press. Somehow the unfamiliar machine broke when she touched it. She was horror-struck:

> There was a lot of yelling and screaming. The foreman said I sabotaged the machine. I became the center of attention, and the thing to be in camp was not to be, and just to blend in. All of a sudden, there were so many people. Everyone was looking at me and blaming me. I was terrified. Somebody went to get Schindler. He inspected it, very seriously, and said I couldn't have sabotaged it. He put me back on a small machine, and from then on, he told them not to put anyone but a man on the big presses.[13]

A similar scare happened to the Danziger brothers. They cracked a press, and someone reported them to the main camp. This time, however, Schindler was out of town. Without *Herr Direktor* to intervene, the men were dragged from Emalia and taken to Plaszow. At the morning roll call the announcement was made that the brothers would be hanged at six o'clock that evening. Everyone was to line up to witness what was done to saboteurs.

Schindler returned only three hours before the scheduled execution. He immediately rushed to the main camp, straight to Goeth's office. No one has said what exchanges took place in the commandant's office, but when Schindler drove back to Emalia, the Danziger brothers were in the back seat of his Mercedes, unharmed.

Schindler would justify these kindnesses to his employees by insisting that his Jews were essential workers. In truth, very few knew anything about enamelware or munitions manufacture. Schindler's prisoners were listed as skilled electricians, tool and die makers, and metal workers. However, most had never worked in these trades. Still, essential workers was the justification he used. However, when he began showing obvious concern for Jews to whom he had no connection, he was in dangerous territory. He risked arrest, imprisonment in a concentration camp, and even death. But his obsession to save as many as he could drove him to increasingly bolder action.

Train to Mauthausen

One of the boldest occurred inside Plaszow. Schindler had just presented Goeth with the gift of a saddle. He had called it an expression of gratitude, but it was in reality a payoff for some favor. He had offered to give Goeth and his new saddle a ride to the commandant's magnificent villa on a hill overlooking the camp. The drive took them past the camp's railroad siding.

This was the station from which transports carried prisoners to the rock quarries of Mauthausen and the gas chambers of Auschwitz. Lately transports were leaving nearly every day. Goeth was systematically weeding out his weakest prisoners to make room for new, stronger Jews from the more recently conquered country of Hungary.

Schindler stopped his Mercedes at the siding. A long line of boxcars waited in the sweltering August sun. They were destined, Goeth said, for Mauthausen. The rejected inmates had stood in the packed cars, the dead and the dying side by side, for three days. One of them described the ordeal: "People began to suffocate. A lot of them became dehydrated, and a lot of them died of thirst and hunger. . . . A lot of people even drank their own urine. . . . The stench was unbearable. It was impossible to move the corpses."[14]

From the car, the two camp operators could hear the moans of the train's occupants, the cries for water. These people meant nothing to Schindler personally except that they were Jews, and he had vowed to save as many Jews as he could. They were headed for certain death, and he could not get them off the train as he had rescued Bankier two years earlier. But perhaps he could make their plight a bit more tolerable. That might be enough to allow some to live through the war.

Turning to Goeth, Schindler asked for permission to hose down the overheated cars. To Goeth, Schindler's concern for these Jews was not only criminally insane, it was also ridiculously useless. But he humored his friend who had given him a beautiful saddle. He ordered the hoses brought.

When the camp's hoses could not reach all the cars, Schindler sent to Emalia for his much longer hoses. He had the doors opened and buckets of water passed to the burning, thirsty prisoners. The bodies of the dead were taken out to make more room for the barely alive. One of the prisoners who hosed down the train was amazed: "He was screaming to the Germans . . . that the Jews are all mechanics, engineers, that the Germans need them, and he guarantees that nobody will escape, to open the doors for them again."[15] In all his miserable days in the camp, the prisoner had never seen anything like this concern for Jews. He said, "To me it was unbelievable: a Nazi with the [party lapel] pin, but no gun or uniform. I said, 'Who is that man?'"[16]

That man was a German whose boldness knew no bounds. Schindler had brought a basket of delicacies when he sent for the hoses: cigarettes, liquor, chocolate. He handed the basket to the train operator who would accompany the transport to the camp in Austria. In full view of several SS officers who had been amused by the scene and Goeth, who merely laughed at his folly, Schindler asked the trainman to stop when he could, to unbolt the cars' doors, and to give the people water. The few survivors of the long trip reported that the trainman did as he had requested.

By the time the train left the siding, in August of 1944, Schindler was running out of ways to help the Jews. He still had important contacts and plenty of money, but the system was getting harder to beat. For several months powers higher than Goeth had been trying to close down Schindler's small subcamp. His weapons section had not yet produced any actual artillery shells, and it was getting harder to show that his was an essential factory. Rumor had it that Plaszow itself might be shut down and its prisoners shipped to Auschwitz.

But Schindler the adventurer was not easily defeated. Schindler the industrialist still had his presses and lathes. And Schindler the protector had a plan.

8

The Listmaker

By the summer of 1944, Germany's defeat was all but certain. On June 6 the western Allies landed in Normandy, France and began a push east. By mid-August the Soviet armies were advancing westward through Poland. The Third Reich was in its final stage.

Fearing he might lose the war, Hitler stepped up his campaign against the Jews. He closed down the forced-labor camps and moved their prisoners to the extermination centers. His henchmen worked furiously to gas as many victims as they could and to burn their bodies, removing any trace of their lives and their deaths.

As the Soviets came farther into German territory, the SS destroyed the evidence of their deeds. The extermination camps in eastern Poland had already been disbanded: Treblinka and Sobibór the previous fall and Belzec a year earlier. The buildings were blown up and trees and flowers planted in their place. The other camps along the path of the Soviet army were also targeted for destruction. Auschwitz, the largest and most efficient of the killing sites, was to remain in operation until the last possible moment.

The Schindler subcamp was ordered closed in September 1944. Schindler could keep only three hundred workers to help him tear down operations. The rest were to be returned to Plaszow to prepare that camp for its demise. Everyone at Emalia wanted to be among the ones to stay with Schindler. One of the lucky ones recalled the competition:

> I was already totally convinced that if there was a future, you had to stay close to Schindler. At one point, Schindler passed in front of me. I stepped up to him— risking my life, because the SS were there, too. I yelled out to him, "Herr Schindler, there are no carpenters left!" What would this have meant to him, I have no idea, but I had to say something. Schindler recognized me evidently, and he put me into the group which remained.[1]

The group that did not remain, that returned to Plaszow, had the unpleasant assignment of destroying any hint of mass murder at the camp. The Soviets, if they got that far, could not be allowed to find out what really happened there. They could not be permitted to discover the bodies from the Krakow ghetto.

Like every other distasteful task, the burden of obliterating evidence was assigned to Jewish inmates. The prisoners dug up thousands of bodies that had been tossed hastily in eleven mass graves. After gold teeth were removed, the gruesome remains were burned on the hill that had been the camp's main execution site. The fires blazed for weeks and the stench lingered for a month. As the ashes drizzled down, Schindler considered the implications for his Jews. Those who removed the remnants of the Nazi crimes were themselves the final witnesses of those atrocities. And Nazis did not let witnesses live.

The Plan

Schindler knew before the burning started that the only way to keep the *Schindlerjuden* alive was to get them out of Plaszow and out of Poland. Before the long-threatened camp closure came, he had been working on a plan. He approached heads of several government departments with a preposterous request: He wanted to keep his camp but move it to a safer location. Even more unbelievably, he asked to take his workers with him.

He trotted out the old arguments. His factory was a war-essential business. Soon it would generate the munitions the army was waiting for. The future of Germany depended on its continued operation. And the workers were necessary too. They were highly skilled specialists, he reasoned. Valuable time would be lost if new workers had to be trained. The seven hundred he had employed at Emalia were not enough, however. He would need three hundred more.

It was an outlandish request and overused logic, but Schindler was determined. And he did not have much time. People were being transported out of Plaszow to Auschwitz every day. He went to Krakow, Warsaw, and Berlin to obtain the necessary authorizations. He reasoned, charmed, begged, and bribed. He brought expensive tokens of his appreciation for those officials who would approve his request. And he brought more gifts for those who understood the urgency of the matter.

Schindler had found the perfect facility in Brinnlitz, near his home town of Zwittau in the Sudetenland of Czechoslovakia. A building that was once part of a textile mill sat vacant. It was large enough for all Emalia's equipment, for offices, for *Herr Direktor's* apartment, and for dormitories for over a thousand prisoners. The plant was near the railroad station, convenient for receiving raw materials and sending out completed artillery shells.

An approval would have to be obtained from the quartermaster general of Brinnlitz. This was not easy, for citizens of this now-German town did not want a prison camp of Jews in their neighborhood. Nor did they want a munitions factory. A weapons factory might draw Allied bombers. Schindler agreed to let his wife approach the quartermaster with his appeal for a permit. Emilie Schindler described the encounter:

> Imagine my surprise when I was confronted by someone whose face looked more and more familiar! Little by little I realized that he was my old swimming teacher. We talked about old times, remembered old stories together, talked about his family and mine, all of which helped me with my request. I asked him for a permit, sealed and signed by him, to set up the munitions factory in Brinnlitz. I left the quartermaster general's premises, permit in hand.[2]

In addition to the Brinnlitz permit, Schindler had obtained signed authorization to take seven hundred men, three hundred women, and one hundred non-Jews from Plaszow to the new camp he would build in Czechoslovakia. He estimated that merely obtaining these documents had cost him 100,000 Reichsmarks—about $40,000.[3]

That, of course, was only the beginning of the costs. Fences, guard towers, homes for guards, and all the other requirements for a camp needed to be constructed. More concrete had to be poured so the floors would support the heavy equipment for munitions manufacture. Despite the expenditures, Schindler had no intention of actually producing munitions. He remained true to the pledge he had made after witnessing the hangings in Plaszow. He would never work for the Germans again. He would design, test, calibrate, and recalibrate, but he would build no artillery shells. His plan was to wait out the war; to hope it ended before anyone discovered that his factory was of absolutely no use to the German war effort.

The List

After the proper permissions were obtained, things moved very quickly. The Soviets had reached Majdanek, the first of the concentration camps to be discovered, before the last six thousand prisoners could be evacuated. The world was beginning to learn the truth. The other camps were in a frantic race to complete their work and self-destruct before the world learned the enormity of the Nazi madness. Time was running out for the *Schindlerjuden*. Schindler set about drawing up a list of the names of the people he would be allowed to take out of Plaszow. He was limited to eleven hundred names.

Exactly how the list was begun is not clear. Schindler probably had the help of Bankier and Stern in recalling the names of his employees. They listed others they could think of from the camp. But there was room for more. Schindler's vow had been to save as many as he could; he had permission to save eleven hundred. He had asked Julius Madritsch, who operated a uniform factory in Plaszow, to bring his factory and workers to Brinnlitz. Madritsch and his manager, Raimund Titsch, had, like Schindler, risked their fortunes and their lives to save the Jews in their employ, but Madritsch declined to move such a distance. However, Titsch added seventy names from the uniform factory to Schindler's growing list. The evening the list was due, Schindler and Titsch made sure they had filled in every space with a name.

But Schindler's list was not the final word. The lists in Plaszow were managed by the camp's labor office, by Marcel Goldberg. Goldberg recognized the importance of this list, and he knew people would pay to be on it. The camp was closing rapidly; transports were leaving regularly. The only possibilities for the desperate prisoners were the Brinnlitz camp or extermination. Goldberg would sell spots on the list to the highest bidders. He would write in a name only in exchange for diamonds. He crossed some names off in order to add those of others. His final act as keeper of the lists was to place his own name on this, the most valuable of all his many lists.

That was not, however, the final list. When the boxcars were ready and the names were read, many people were angry to find their names missing. Some, not realizing what Goldberg had done, thought Schindler had forgotten them. Others had paid to be put on the list, only to be knocked off by someone with more diamonds. On the trip to the new camp, it was discovered that the list had been left in Plaszow. Because the convoy of railcars included other people also, Goldberg was required to create the list again, from memory. Goeth's former secretary, Mietek Pemper, insisted on helping Goldman type. He saw to it that some of the original names made it back on the list.

The Schindler list was the last ray of hope, the last chance of life for any in Plaszow. Nearly all of the twenty-five thousand prisoners whose names were not on the list perished, most in the gas chambers of Auschwitz.

Sidetracked

Those on the list left in two shifts: the men on October 15 and the women a week later. Neither group, however, went

Mietek Pemper was Polish, born in Krakow on March 24, 1920, but he had a German grandmother. She taught him the German language.

Because of his knowledge of German as well as Polish, Pemper became the translator for the German authorities in Krakow. In Plaszow, he was the interpreter and a typist for Amon Goeth. As a typist, he saw many secret Nazi documents. He thought his life was in constant danger because he knew so much about Nazi plans and activities. Endowed with a phenomenal memory, Pemper memorized many of the precise and incriminating figures in some of the reports.

German soldiers in the Soviet Union needed a constant supply of war materials. Schindler knew he could keep his Jewish workers safe as long as he was helping the war effort.

Pemper was a help to Schindler in a number of ways. He suggested to Schindler that manufacturing shell casings for weapons was the only way he could continue to employ and shelter Jews. He helped type Schindler's list of people who could go from Plaszow to Brinnlitz.

After liberation, Pemper took care of his mother, an Auschwitz survivor, in Poland until her death in 1958. He gave testimony at the trial of Amon Goeth and others. Because of Pemper's excellent memory, Goeth was convicted.

After the release of the film *Schindler's List*, he gave lectures about his experiences. He advocated German-Israeli and Christian-Jewish cooperation and was awarded the Order of Merit from the University of Augsburg.[4]

directly to Brinnlitz. The plans for Plaszow's closure called for male prisoners to go to Gröss-Rosen and females to Auschwitz. Auschwitz was selected because it was nearby and the largest of the killing centers. Gröss-Rosen was one hundred fifty miles further west, in Germany. It would be one of the last camps to remain open. When the advance of the Soviet army forced the SS to abandon Auschwitz, its gas chambers were shipped to Gröss-Rosen. Schindler's new camp was actually a subcamp of Gröss-Rosen. The people on Schindler's list were taken, along with other Plaszow evacuees, to these two camps. From there other trains would take them to Brinnlitz.

The eight hundred men of Schindler's list spent three excruciating days in Gröss-Rosen. It was during these three days that Goldberg had to revise the list. One of the men described the frightening experience:

> We arrived at Gröss-Rosen late in the afternoon. We saw the chimneys of the crematoria burning. We weren't so sure we were going to Schindler. We were kept outside all night for a very exact body search, even internal. We were naked all night on a very cold late October night. I got my clothes at eleven o'clock the next morning. The first sign that we were going to Schindler was that they put us in a special barracks. The conditions were so cramped that nobody could sleep.[5]

When the nightmare was over, eight hundred men were packed into cattle cars. They were given five ounces of bread and taken the one hundred miles to Brinnlitz. The trip took two days.

The women were not as fortunate. As dreadful as Plaszow had been, Auschwitz was unimaginably worse. One survivor recalled her first impression of the camp:

It was bitter cold, rainy, miserable, filthy, mud up to your ankles. The latrines were overflowing. And they made us stand to be counted for long periods of time. We stood in fives, so we took turns being in the middle. They had fur coats on, and we were naked. And hungry! All we got was water with a few vegetables in it.[6]

The cold was only part of the terror. Another woman was stunned by the shadow of the crematoria: "The first thing that struck me was the terrible stench, and the smoke so heavy you could feel it. The ashes were landing on you. Your eyes were burning. You could taste it."[7]

But the cold and the ashes could not compare with the panic the three hundred women felt when they thought they were going to die. One of Oskar's first Jewish employees, who had been with him since the days of the ghetto, remembered: "You can imagine how scared we were. We knew we were not in Brinnlitz: We were in that hell. They took us to a shower. We thought we were going already to the gas. We had to undress, and they pushed [us] in naked. We thought it was the last moment of our lives." [8]

Those torturous moments were to drag on for weeks. For some unexplained reason, the women on Schindler's list were lost in the Auschwitz bureaucracy. Unfortunately, Schindler was not able to rescue them. He was in a Gestapo prison.

Third Arrest

In the past, Schindler's run-ins with the Nazi police had been for crimes he had committed. This time it was for another's misdeeds. In the last months of Plaszow, Amon Goeth had been arrested. Not for the brutality or wanton killing of which he was obviously guilty. He was accused of profiting from his position by selling camp food and supplies on the black market. In the course of that investigation, the Gestapo had caught him with eighty thousand Reichsmarks for which he could not account. He said Schindler had given them to him "to go easy on the Jews."[9]

Schindler was in prison for eight days before he could give a satisfactory answer. The money was a loan, he explained, given to Goeth to expedite moving his workers from Plaszow to Schindler's camp. These highly skilled workers were needed for his war-essential production, he said, repeating his oft-used argument. He could not afford to have the process slowed; Germany could not afford it. So he paid Goeth to speed things up. When the interrogators appeared to believe him, Schindler was so bold as to ask for his loan back.

But it was probably not the tired logic that saved Schindler. As usual, it was most likely his connections. When he was arrested he had asked his wife to call his Emalia secretary so she could cancel his appointments. And the secretary had called the high-placed people who, on two earlier occasions, had cancelled his appointment with the Gestapo.

Auschwitz

When he returned to Brinnlitz, Schindler learned that the women were still in Auschwitz. The men of his factory begged him to intervene somehow. Intervention usually meant a bribe. And three hundred women would be expensive. But Schindler never balked at the price of his Jews. He sent someone to the extermination camp with gifts to secure their release.

Stern said the emissary was one of Schindler's beautiful secretaries. Emilie Schindler said it was a childhood friend who worked for the German army. Some said it was a female SS officer. People have speculated that the bribe was food and liquor, or a bag of diamonds, or possibly sexual favors. Yad Vashem, the Holocaust remembrance and documentation authority of Israel, says it was the promise of a payment of seven Reichsmarks per day per prisoner.[10] Whatever the arrangement, it was only partially successful. Schindler had to go to Auschwitz himself.

The camp personnel were willing to give him three hundred women, but they did not want to bother with any list, any specific names. But Schindler had men back at Brinnlitz who were waiting for their wives, mothers, and daughters. He wanted his three hundred. After all, they were skilled munitions workers. The Auschwitz guards countered that children's names were on the list, and children could not be skilled artisans.

Giving an argument he had used before, Schindler explained that these particular children had exceptionally long fingers. They were essential because their small hands could polish the insides of his artillery shells. Whether they agreed or were simply worn down, the SS released everyone Schindler asked for. Yad Vashem observed that "this is the only recorded case in the history of the extermination camp that such a large group of people were allowed to leave alive while the gas chambers were still in operation."[11]

When the women, tattered and weak, arrived in Brinnlitz, they were met by a contingent of SS men. But standing head and shoulders above Josef Liepold, the camp's commandant, was Oskar Schindler. He welcomed the numbed women with a smile and a promise: "When you go inside the building, you'll find soup and bread waiting for you. You have nothing more to worry about. You're with me now."[12]

When he was not with them, however, there was cause to worry. And he was frequently gone. He continued to buy and sell on the black market, so while Bankier and Stern ran the factory, he often drove to Krakow, Brno, and other cities.

He was on such a trip the day Liepold came to the factory looking for children. Commandants of all the subcamps of Gröss-Rosen had received orders to send any children who may be in the camps to Auschwitz. Dr. Josef Mengele, notorious for his dispassionate cruelty, wanted them for medical experiments.

Schindler was not there to charm, bluff, or bribe Liepold out of his assignment. The few children at Brinnlitz had felt no need to hide, so Liepold's search found them easily. They and their fathers were taken by passenger train to Auschwitz just as their mothers were boarding cattle cars to come to Brinnlitz. Because the war was nearing its end, some survived. But Schindler could not save them; he could not save everyone. But he would do what he could. And this was more than most people even attempted to do.

Doing What He Could

One thing Oskar Schindler could do was supplement the meager store of food the camp was given. In the alleys and back rooms of the cities of occupied Czechoslovakia and Poland he exchanged pots and pans for flour, bread, and vegetables. He bought gasoline and cigarettes for the camp and liquor for bribes. Once he made a three-hundred-mile trip carrying two flasks of vodka and returning with the same two flasks filled with medicine.

These items were rationed, so getting them was not easy. Transporting them to Brinnlitz required permits he did not have. These difficulties did not stop Schindler. In his employ was Moshe Bejski, a draftsman who had forged Aryan papers in the ghetto. Schindler managed to get hold of one permit and Bejski copied it perfectly. With a piece of rubber and a razor blade, the prisoner carved a stamp that would be put on

Moshe Bejski, *Schindler's Forger*

Born near Krakow, Poland in 1920, Bejski was an accomplished forger by the age of twenty. In the Krakow ghetto, he forged Aryan papers for Jewish girls seeking jobs in Germany. In Plaszow, he worked in the registration office. That put him in a position to help Stern deliver money from the Joint Distribution Committee.

Bejski got on Schindler's list as a draftsman, a technical designer. At Brinnlitz, he drew blueprints and counterfeited official documents. He and his two brothers were saved by Oskar Schindler.

After the war, Bejski emigrated to Israel. In the 1960s, he gave testimony in the Adolf Eichmann trial. He became a judge in Israel's Constitutional Court, then in the new nation's Supreme Court. As a member of the Commission of the Righteous, he helped set the criteria for being named a Righteous Gentile and determined who fit the criteria. He served as president of the commission

Adolf Eichmann (pictured) was convicted and sentenced to hang. Moshe Bejski's testimony helped to bring about the conviction.

until 1995. He helped create the Avenue and the Garden of the Righteous, where Righteous Gentiles are honored with trees planted in their names.

Bejski said, "If Schindler had been a normal man, he would not have done what he did. Everything he did put him in danger. He could have done much less and still have qualified as one of the righteous."[13]

all of Schindler's purchases and travel documents, making them official government business.

As dangerous as they sometimes were, Schindler's travels were not as perilous as life inside the camp. Liepold and his SS staff were not as ruthless as Goeth, but they were still agents of Nazi Germany who had sworn allegiance to Hitler. They did not simply shoot people for small infractions as Goeth had done; they arrested, tried, and executed them in a more formal manner. What Schindler could do was try to control the formal proceedings.

That is how he saved Janek Dresser. Janek was young, only nineteen, and knew nothing of metal work. He had learned how to operate a lathe reasonably well, but his German foreman moved him to a press. Unfamiliar with the heavy machine, Janek managed to short out the wiring and crack a plate. The infuriated Liepold commanded an immediate trial. If found guilty of sabotage, Dresser would be hanged in full view of the entire camp. Schindler insisted on running the hearing.

As the shaken youth tried to defend himself, Schindler appeared as harsh as Liepold and his associate. With an angry scowl, *Herr Direktor* ordered Janek to chronicle exactly how he had damaged his expensive machine. Part way through the boy's faltering explanation, Schindler stopped him. He made him repeat himself as though he had just admitted to an unbelievably idiotic blunder. Then he stomped up to him and smacked him hard across his face.

"The stupidity of you . . . people!" he yelled. "I can't believe it!" Then he winked at his employee before turning back to the SS men. "I wish they were intelligent enough to sabotage a machine," he moaned. "Then at least I'd have their . . . hides! But what can you do with these people? They're an utter waste of time."[14]

In what seemed like a fit of rage, he ordered Janek out of his sight. He told the SS men to forget the entire incident, and he invited them to his apartment for drinks. Thus he dismissed the incident and saved his prisoner from execution. The SS men may not have been satisfied, but they did not argue.

Schindler tried to keep the guards at Brinnlitz on the perimeter, in their towers, away from his workers. But he could not stop the inspections that seemed to be more and more frequent. What he could do was charm the inspectors with food and drink and blur their vision with vodka or schnapps. On one occasion a very tipsy SS officer had difficulty leaving Schindler's office. As the inspector teetered at the top of a staircase, Schindler gave in to emotions that had been building up since he witnessed the slaughter in the ghetto. Whether he tripped or pushed the man is not certain, but the officer landed at the bottom of the steps with a great bloody gash on his head. Believing that Schindler had shot him, the shaken man cursed him loudly. As he left, with his inspection undone, he threatened: "You will not live until any liberation, Schindler. Don't think you fool us. You belong in a concentration camp yourself, along with all your Jews!"[15]

The Frozen Transport

Schindler was not alone in helping the *Schindlerjuden* in Brinnlitz. Even though he still had mistresses, Emilie Schindler was a faithful wife who shared her husband's concern for his Jews. She also did what she could. She made some of the black-market runs for Schindler and secured grain from a nearby mill. She oversaw the kitchen and she tended the sick. Workers remember her being very kind, occasionally bringing them packets of food in addition to their camp meals.

She and Schindler could also provide some reassurances to their endangered employees. The couple had a grand villa in the town of Brinnlitz, away from the camp. But they did not spend a single night there. Instead, they stayed in a small apartment at the factory so their workers would not fear surprise nighttime inspections. Emilie Schindler's grandest hour, however, was spent helping the condemned Jews of the frozen transport.

The two cattle cars had left Goleszow, a subcamp of Auschwitz, in January 1945. The huge camp and all its satellites were being shut down. One hundred twenty inmates were locked inside the cars with no food or water and sent west, away from the advancing Russian army. But at every station they stopped, every camp, no one wanted the Jewish prisoners. After ten days, someone heard the sounds of human scratching coming from inside the abandoned cars. That person called Schindler and asked if he wanted to take the two cars. Oskar had vowed he would save as many as he could. So he accepted the orphan train.

When the cars arrived on the Brinnlitz siding, a heavy snow was falling. In the below zero temperature, the locks on the doors had frozen shut. Poldek Pfefferberg, now a prisoner in the Schindler camp, brought a blowtorch from the welding equipment. Others brought axes. The inmates burned straw beneath the cars to melt the ice. When that was too slow, Schindler told them to use some mattresses instead. "Tomorrow you get new," he promised.[16]

Jewish laborers build Oskar Schindler's armaments factory in Brinnlitz.

When the doors were finally pried open, a gruesome picture was revealed. Emilie Schindler was haunted for years by the sight:

> The spectacle I saw was a nightmare almost beyond imagination. It was impossible to distinguish the men from the women: they were all so emaciated, . . . weighing under seventy pounds most of them, they looked like skeletons. Their eyes were shining like glowing coals in the dark.[17]

Thirteen were dead; three more survived for only a few hours. The rest were black with frostbite. But they were alive. The workers cleared a room in the factory, spread straw on the floor, and turned it into an infirmary. Emilie and a small group of prisoners moved among the frozen bodies, feeding them tiny spoonfuls of porridge. She made black-market runs to purchase medicines. She gave up her jewelry in exchange for food and vitamins.

The commandant was incensed that one hundred and four people with no economic value were being nursed back to life. Schindler assured him that, once they were well, they would prove to be skilled workers. Throughout the months it took them to recover, he paid the German government the daily labor fee for each of them. Even though they contributed nothing to Schindler or the war effort, he paid the same for them as for his other workers.

The commandant tried to put his foot down, however, when it came to the sixteen corpses. Even without crematoria, all the concentration camps were required to burn their dead. Cremation was abhorrent to Jews, and Schindler had come to care about their concerns as well as their lives. He purchased ground near a Catholic cemetery and he bought the silence of the commandant. The sixteen Goleszow bodies, as well as those of two inmates who had died in Brinnlitz, were buried with full Jewish religious services in that ground.

In Trouble

Although the commandant begrudgingly allowed Schindler such kindnesses, he had another issue with the wily industrialist. The reason Schindler had been permitted to operate a camp was to produce secret weapons for the German army. Oskar had promised to design and manufacture artillery shells. But in its five years in Zablocie and seven months in Brinnlitz, the camp had delivered no workable shells. The nonproduction was deliberate, part of Schindler's vow to beat the system.

Manufacturing faulty weapons was easy. Machines could be calibrated so that their end products were defective. Fooling the inspectors was also fairly simple. Furnace gauges could be manipulated so they registered one temperature but performed at another. Stern claimed that Schindler bought shells from other manufacturers and kept them on hand just for inspections.

Placating the higher-ups was becoming increasingly difficult. The Brinnlitz shells were not final products. The Armaments Inspectorate had parts manufactured in different camps in case the Allies bombed one camp. One camp made the shells, another inserted the fuses, and a third packed them with explosives. Schindler's products repeatedly failed quality control, so the other camps could not do their jobs. The excuses of startup problems and poor equipment were wearing thin.

As complaints mounted, Schindler was finding it harder and harder to beat the system.

9

The Displaced Person

By the beginning of 1945, few people doubted that Germany would lose the war. It was only a matter of time. The end of the war meant an end to the camps, an end to the butchering of Jews. But for Oskar Schindler, it meant the beginning of other problems—for his Jews and for himself. For the Jews, it meant almost certain death. If the Soviets drew near Brinnlitz, the commandant had orders to march all his prisoners to Mauthausen and shoot any who could not make the journey. For Schindler, it could also mean death. Rumor had it that the approaching Russian soldiers were killing Germans. And the Czechs were poised to take revenge on any Germans for the atrocities they had suffered in 1938.

Preparing for Liberation

Schindler tried to prevent both eventualities. He began to acquire arms: rifles, revolvers, automatic weapons, and hand grenades. Some he got from the SS police chief of Brinnlitz's province. He told him that he needed to protect his factory. Prisoners could revolt or Russians could storm the gates. Schindler convinced him with these arguments and a diamond ring.

Then he appointed one of the prisoners to train some of the others in how to use the weapons. Several of the inmates had served in the Polish army and figured out quickly how the more modern guns operated. Schindler connected a small group of his Jews with the Czech underground, from whom they received more weapons. They stored their arsenal under bales of wire in an electrical transformer station. The prisoners were to use the guns to defend themselves if that proved necessary.

In addition to the weapons, Schindler had a storage room crammed with shoes, thread, wool, and fabric. The German navy had needed a place to store these items. Schindler had bought the contract, which allowed him to stash away eighteen truckloads of goods. He estimated their value at $150,000. After the war, he reasoned, when his prisoners were free, they could use the materials to clothe themselves and begin their lives anew.

They would also need goods they could trade for food once the factory's stores were depleted. They had to have something to sustain them on their journeys home. In his storeroom he set aside a bottle of vodka and two hundred cigarettes for each prisoner.

Once Schindler prepared militarily and economically for liberation, he tried to prepare the *Schindlerjuden* psychologically. He used the occasion of his thirty-seventh birthday, April 28, 1945. It was two days before Adolf Hitler committed suicide. As was his custom, Schindler had a big party, celebrating with extra bread for every worker and plenty of liquor for himself. At the end of the party, he made a speech. Its purpose was to warn the guards and encourage the Jews. He told them that the war would soon be over. And he promised to remain at the camp until that time—but only five minutes longer.

Ten days later, the war ended. The surrender was announced in the early hours of May 7. Hostilities were to cease at midnight the evening of May 8. Schindler had Winston Churchill's victory speech broadcast over the factory's loudspeakers. Few of the prisoners could speak English, but they knew instinctively what the strange words meant. Helen Sternlicht Rosenzweig, Amon Goeth's former maid, remembered listening to the message:

> We could hear on the speakers that something was very exciting. We didn't understand, but we knew it was a voice of power, and Schindler let us listen. I realized this must be the end of the war. It was a feeling of, we are free! Goeth came to my mind right away: He can never come for me anymore.[1]

What they did understand was that their lives would completely change. Exactly how they would change they were not sure. Would the guards kill them in obedience to their dead Führer? Would the Russian liberators abuse them? What about the Czechs . . . did they hate Jews? All they knew was that the next day, at five minutes past midnight, their protector would leave them.

At midnight Oskar Schindler would become a wanted man. He was a Nazi war criminal, a slave-labor camp operator. He had no choice but to flee. He could not charm or bribe the Soviet army. His only hope was to make his way to American soldiers. They had a reputation for being humane.

Helen Sternlicht Rosenzweig, *Goeth's Maid*

When she was only seventeen, three days after arriving at Plaszow in 1943, Helen Sternlicht was chosen by Amon Goeth to be his maid. She risked her life many times by sneaking food to her mother and sisters in Plaszow, giving SS documents from Goeth's files to camp resistance fighters, and protecting others from Goeth's sadistic outbursts. Schindler personally placed Helen's name, along with the names of her two sisters, on his list of people going to Brinnlitz. Her testimony after the war helped convict Goeth, who was executed for his crimes.

After liberation, Helen went to Austria. She married Josef Jonas, another Brinnlitz survivor. With her husband and her sisters, she emigrated to the United States. Josef died in 1980, and in 1990 Helen married Henry Rosenzweig, another Holocaust survivor.

After release of the film *Schindler's List*, Helen was asked to make many public appearances to speak about her experiences. She accepted, saying "It was meant for me to speak for all the people that perished." Of Schindler, she said, "I realized that all the times he spoke to me and comforted me, he meant it. . . . I realized he was like a double agent. I felt safe."[2]

Now it was the *Schindlerjuden's* turn to do what they could for their savior.

Preparing for Flight

In the two days between the announcement and the war's official end, the factory workers prepared for Schindler's departure. They readied his car. Very carefully they peeled back the upholstery from the Mercedes' door and slipped bags of diamonds in the empty spaces. Schindler had reserved these small bags for his escape. After all, he too would need something with which to begin his life again.

The prisoners also drew up a letter. Written in both German and Hebrew, it testified that Schindler had saved their lives. It told the reader, whoever that might be, that he was a good man and deserved whatever help he needed. They hoped it would be enough to keep him from being shot.

All the inmates wanted to do more. Oskar Schindler had snatched them from certain death, had kept them alive; had held their families together. They wanted to give him some remembrance, some sign of their appreciation. What could they give? They had nothing that Schindler had not given them. A jeweler among the prisoners suggested that they had their craftsmanship, their ability to create. He would make a ring.

The material was furnished by Szymon Jereth, the man who had supplied the lumber for Schindler's first act of defiance. He still had gold teeth—at least enough for a ring that would fit one of Schindler's big fingers. A prisoner who had been a dentist extracted the gold. Among the furnaces intended for weapons production, the jeweler melted the gold and fashioned a plain ring. He inscribed it to Oskar Schindler, with all their thanks and a verse from the Talmud, part of

116

their sacred writings: "He who saves a single life saves the world."[3]

The ring had not been finished long before Schindler assembled his Jews on the factory floor. The SS officers were there, too. It was six o'clock; the war would not be over for six more hours. But before he left them he wanted to do as he had on his birthday. He wanted to frighten the guards so they would not kill the prisoners. He also wanted to encourage the inmates to avoid bringing further hardship upon themselves. "My children," he began, "you are saved. Germany has lost the war."[4] He continued:

> After six years of the cruel murder of human beings . . . Europe is now trying to return to peace and order. I would like to turn to you for unconditional order and discipline—to all of you who together with me have worried through many hard years—in order that you can live through the present and . . . go back to your destroyed and plundered homes. . . . The fact that millions among you . . . have been liquidated has been disapproved by thousands of Germans. . . . In the new Europe there will be . . . incorruptible judges, who will listen to you. . . . Don't go into the neighboring houses to rob and plunder. . . . Refrain from any individual acts of revenge and terror. . . . Don't thank me for your survival. Thank your people who worked day and night to save you from extermination.[5]

After the speech, the SS guards left the building. Like Schindler, they would soon be considered criminals. Killing twelve hundred people in the waning hours of the war would be pointless for them. Escaping the Russians and getting back to Germany made much more sense.

Schindler also needed to escape. He bid his crew *Auf Wiedersehen* (good-bye) and he and Emilie Schindler went to their apartment to pack. Some of the Jews stopped them,

After the war, Allied soldiers forced local residents near concentration and death camps to exhume the bodies of Holocaust victims. The soldiers did this so the residents could see what they had allowed to happen.

presenting their gift and their letter. Schindler was genuinely moved and grateful. Many of the Jews were in tears, excited that their long ordeal was over but frightened about what life without Schindler would be like. "We were hysterical when he left," one said. "He was like a father!"[6]

Escape

True to his word, Schindler did not depart the camp until five minutes past midnight on the morning of May 9. He and his wife were both dressed in the striped, pajama-like uniform of prisoners. They were accompanied by eight inmates who had volunteered to go with them. One drove the Mercedes with the Schindlers, the others drove a truck laden with liquor and cigarettes that could be traded for food and lodging. The plan was to pose as prisoners escaped from a labor camp in the camp *Direktor's* car. With the Schindlers' obviously Aryan features, the ruse was risky. But they had no other option.

The tiny convoy was a small part of a mass exodus from Czechoslovakia. German soldiers and German civilians were all hurrying to their Fatherland. The war was over but the Soviet soldiers on their heels were angry. Thirteen million of their brothers had died in battle. Seven million of their civilians had been massacred by *Einsatzgruppen* or killed in concentration camps. Every German was running from the advancing Soviet army. Emilie Schindler described the harrowing flight:

> All along the road, over and over again, there were the same horrible scenes of people trying to flee, surrounded by a spectacle worthy of Dante's *Inferno*, of German tanks scattered in the lonely fields, each exploding in the midst of a gigantic blaze.[7]

When they reached the first town, they were stopped by armed Czechs. They had to surrender their only weapon, but the Czechs seemed to believe their story. They pointed them to a Red Cross office in the town's center. The relief workers suggested that escaped prisoners would be safest in the police station. So the eight Jews and two Germans spent their first night of freedom in the unlocked cells of the town jail.

The next morning they discovered that their cars had been ransacked and torn apart. Gone were not only the diamonds, but also the tires, the engines, and everything else of value. All they owned now were in the suitcases they had taken with them. Fortunately Schindler had some money in his suitcase. That allowed the refugees to board a train. They rode it until they came to a forest on the Austrian border. Then they walked, not sure where they were going or what they would find when they arrived.

What they found in the forest was a company of American soldiers. One of the prisoners spoke English and risked telling the Americans the truth: They were Jews and the Schindlers were Germans. The gamble paid off. This company had a number of Jewish soldiers and a Jewish chaplain. The rabbi read Schindler's letter from his workers and wept. As he relayed the information written in Hebrew, the soldiers clapped, hugged, and cried. These were the first concentration camp survivors they had encountered.

The Americans fed the little party well for two days. They gave them a German ambulance they had captured and sent them on their way. The ten spent the next several months looking for a home. The Schindlers eventually made it to Munich, Germany.

Displaced Person

All of Schindler's diamonds were gone. The vodka and cigarettes had been spent. The one-time millionaire had absolutely nothing. Two of his former prisoners, Henry and

120

Poldek Rosner, had a small apartment in Munich. They had jobs playing musical instruments in a restaurant. They took in their penniless former savior.

After the war, displaced persons (DP) centers sprang up throughout Europe. They were for people who had no home to which to return. Many were physically and psychologically unable to return to a normal life. Some spent years in displaced persons centers. Oskar Schindler did not go to a DP camp. But he was truly a displaced person. He had lost his home, his business, even his country. He was no longer welcome in Czechoslovakia, Poland, or Germany. The United States refused him admittance because he had been a Nazi. The only people who were family to him were his *Schindlerjuden*.

In 1949, the Jewish Joint Distribution Committee came to his rescue. This was the American group to which he reported on the barbaric treatment of the Jews of Krakow. The organization gave him $15,000 and passage to Argentina. The Schindlers sailed to begin a new life in South America. Ever generous, he took some of the *Schindlerjuden* with him. And ever the womanizer, he also took a new lover.

But his new life quickly soured. The only business opportunities in Argentina were in farming, and Schindler did not like to be tied down to a routine. He bought a truckload of nutria, otter-like animals valued for their fur, and began a nutria ranch. But the enterprise was going bankrupt in 1957, and the couple needed more money. While Emilie Schindler worked to salvage the business, Oskar Schindler went back to Germany to receive a small compensation from the government for the loss of his Brinnlitz factory. He never returned to Argentina.

Oskar Schindler at a reunion in Munich, Germany, in 1946 with some of the *Schindlerjuden*.

In Frankfurt, Germany, Schindler remained a displaced person. He was out of place politically. He gave testimony against some of his old SS drinking companions, which was not popular in postwar Germany. He identified Liepold and catalogued the crimes of several Plaszow men. He did not attend Amon Goeth's trial and execution as there were plenty of other willing witnesses.

Oskar Schindler was a displaced person socially. People spat at him on the streets, threw stones, and called him a Jew-lover. He was out of place financially. He began a cement company, but it folded in 1961. Another venture also failed. According to a reporter, his business partner pulled out of the arrangement saying, "I am a Nazi and now it is clear that you are a friend of Jews and I will not work together with you any more."[8] Continually short of funds, he even sold the ring that had been forged in Brinnlitz—for schnapps. The only place he was truly comfortable was with the families of the Jews he had rescued.

Rescuing the Rescuer

Those Jews never forgot that they owed their lives to him. In 1961, a number of them paid his way to visit them in Israel. Two hundred twenty people he had saved greeted him enthusiastically. At least once a year until the day he died the *Schindlerjuden* brought him to Israel. They treated him to fine hotels, expensive meals, and excellent liquor. The Jews who had moved to the United States and other countries flew him to their homes to help them celebrate weddings and anniversaries.

But when he returned to Frankfurt, there was only a tiny apartment and simple food. He had no relatives. According to rumor, he had two children through his affairs, but they were not part of his life.[9] He was completely alone. His friends saw

123

that he was discouraged, lonely, and disillusioned. In response, a group of *Schindlerjuden* began contributing to his support. They also petitioned the German government, which finally awarded him a small pension in 1968. The money never lasted very long. Moshe Bejski, the Brinnlitz forger, remarked, "If we sent \$3,000–\$4,000, he spent it within two or three weeks, then phoned to say he didn't have a penny. He spent money quicker than we could raise it."[10]

But that was Oskar Schindler. And his Jews did not resent him for it. They knew he would always love wealth, women, and whiskey. But they also knew he loved them. He asked about their children, wrote them letters, came to their events. When he had money he gave them lavish presents.

Besides, they owed him a debt they could never adequately repay. They focused on that rather than on his drinking, womanizing, or spending. They were aware of his faults, many and large though they were, but whenever they spoke of those flaws there was always a *but*.

He "was a big mixture of everything," Irene Hirschfeld said, "*but* we only saw the good side of him."[11]

"He took chances. He was a gambler," Lewis Fagen admitted. *But*, "if he hadn't been what he was, he wouldn't have done what he did."[12]

"Schindler liked money, girls, alcohol," Victor Lewis would say. *But* "Here is the point: Schindler risked his life and his fortune in order to save the people under his power."[13]

"I am aware of who Schindler was," Moshe Bejski declared, "*but* without Schindler most of those 1,200 Jews would not have remained alive."[14]

Poldek Pfefferberg, one of his staunchest supporters, summed up the feelings of the *Schindlerjuden* who continued for years to pay his bills and shower him with gifts and praise:

"He was a very wealthy man, a multimillionaire. He could have taken the money and gone to Switzerland. . . . He could have bought Beverly Hills. *But* instead, he gambled his life and all of his money to save us."[15]

On October 9, 1974, Oskar Schindler died in Frankfurt, Germany. As was his wish, he was buried in Israel, in a Catholic cemetery in Jerusalem. More than four hundred of his Jews and their families attended the burial, weeping in sadness and thanksgiving.

Among the Righteous

The story of Oskar Schindler's rescue of more than twelve hundred Jews went largely untold for sixteen years. And even then it was only known among Holocaust survivors. The world at large would not learn the amazing tale for another two decades.

The first to write of Oskar's deeds was Herbert Steinhouse, a Canadian journalist. He interviewed both Itzhak Stern and Schindler himself just four years after the war ended. When his agent tried to get his article published, however, the world was tired of Holocaust stories.

People were interested again in the 1960s, stimulated by the highly publicized case of Adolf Eichmann, a notorious Nazi war criminal. Eichmann was found in 1960, tried in Israel in 1961, and executed in 1962. While the trial was going on, Schindler came to Israel for the first time. Hungry for news about Eichmann, a London newspaper printed a story comparing the actions of the two Nazis. Articles appeared in German papers in the next few years. But none of these received wide circulation.

They did, however, catch the attention of a filmmaker. The giant Metro-Goldwyn-Mayer began to develop a movie based on Schindler's wartime activities. The production company even gave Oskar a hefty advance. But in 1966, work on the film was cancelled and nothing came of it. A German television documentary appeared in 1973, but it was not seen outside Germany.

Getting the Story Told

One of Schindler's Jews was determined that the story would be told. Poldek Pfefferberg, Oskar's black-market supplier in the Krakow ghetto, had made a vow. Just after the war, when he and his wife were safe in Munich, Germany, he promised himself that he would see to it that the world would learn what happened in Krakow, in Zablocie, and in Brinnlitz. He told Schindler, "You protect us, you save us, you feed us— we survived the Holocaust, the tragedy, the hardship, the sickness, the beatings, the killings! We must tell your story!"[1]

For more than thirty years he tried his best to keep that promise. Living in the United States under the Americanized name Leopold Page, he opened a leather goods store in Beverly Hills. His customers were people the public would listen to: actors, writers, producers, agents. They could write best-selling books or make blockbuster movies. He tried to interest anyone and everyone who came through his shop's doors in the story of a German industrialist who saved twelve hundred Jews. For thirty years no one listened seriously.

Then, in 1980, an Australian writer named Thomas Keneally needed a new briefcase. In Page's store he heard the story for the first time, and it captivated him. With Page's

127

help, he gathered documents, names, and phone numbers. He interviewed fifty *Schindlerjuden* in seven countries. The result, in 1982, was exactly what Leopold had hoped: a detailed, well researched, accurate best seller.

But there was more. Movie director Steven Spielberg read Keneally's book. He asked Page to help him turn it into a film. It was eleven years before he started production. Page called the director's office once a week for those eleven years, trying to coax him to begin. Referring to Spielberg's *Gremlins*, Page would say, "enough with the little furry animals."[2] When the movie, *Schindler's List*, was made and released in 1993, the world finally saw the true story of Oskar Schindler's unusual heroism.

Honoring Schindler

With the truth came the recognition heroes deserve. The *Schindlerjuden* found ways, large and small, to honor their savior. Three of them, Abraham Zuckerman, Murray Pantirer, and Isak Levenstein, found a unique way to pay tribute to Oskar Schindler. They formed a partnership building housing developments. In each subdivision, they named one street after him. In more than twenty cities throughout New Jersey and Pennsylvania there is a Schindler Drive, a Schindler Court, or a Schindler Plaza. Their children have carried on the tradition.

The three partners also found a way to honor Schindler in Jerusalem, Israel. That city is home to Hebrew University. Part of the university is the Harry S. Truman Research Institute for the Advancement of Peace. By contacting seventy-five other *Schindlerjuden*, the three men raised $120,000 in 1972 to dedicate a floor of the research institute to Oskar Schindler.

Perhaps the greatest honor was the result of the efforts of the prisoner who had made documents for Oskar at Brinnlitz. Moshe Bejski, the one-time forger, had become a well respected judge in Israel. He was one of a small committee of people charged with identifying non-Jews who risked their lives to save Jews from certain death during the Holocaust. Such people were recognized as Righteous Gentiles, or Righteous Among the Nations. The title was bestowed by Yad Vashem, the Holocaust Martyrs' and Heroes' Remembrance Center. It is the highest honor Israel can give a non-Jew. On April 28, 1962, his fifty-fourth birthday, Oskar Schindler was declared a Righteous Gentile.

Righteous Gentiles are each invited to plant a carob tree along the Avenue of the Righteous or in the Garden of the Righteous at Yad Vashem in Jerusalem. Schindler's tree stands as a living remembrance of his deeds. Like all Righteous Gentiles, he was awarded a medal with an inscription from the Talmud. It is the same message that appeared on the ring his grateful children had given him: "Whosoever preserves one life—it is as though he has preserved the entire world."[3]

Unlike Other Righteous

Oskar Schindler stands out among the 20,205 people declared Righteous Gentiles. Some acted from religious conviction; Schindler had long ago abandoned any religious observance or duty. Some of the Righteous were in positions of political influence; Schindler was a Nazi with no authority. Some saved Jews for whom they felt some personal responsibility, those they loved; Schindler rescued people whose names he did not even know. Some could hide people away because they lived on the edges of the terror; Schindler sheltered hundreds in the very center of the Holocaust. He does not fit into any normal category of rescuer.

Born in June 1925 in Krakow, Poland, Pantirer refers to himself as a "schlepper," or an unimportant person. At Plaszow, he worked in the kitchen, where he met up with his childhood friend Abe Zuckerman.

Pantirer does not know how he got on Schindler's list. Somehow he went to Brinnlitz as a metalworker, a trade he knew nothing about. The list saved his life. He was the only one from his family of nine to survive the Holocaust.

After the war, Pantirer spent three and a half years in a displaced persons camp. He married Lucy and emigrated to the United States on January 17, 1949. He began a building development company with his uncle Isak Levenstein and his good friend Abe Zuckerman. The three built the company into a great success and made a fortune. They named one street in every subdivision they developed after Oskar Schindler.

The United States Holocaust Memorial Museum is located at 100 Raoul Wallenberg Place in Washington, D.C. Raoul Wallenberg was a Swedish diplomat who rescued thousands of Jews from the Nazis.

Pantirer helped support Oskar and Emilie Schindler financially. He serves on a number of boards and councils, many having to do with preserving the memory of the Holocaust. He is a founding member of the United States Holocaust Memorial Museum.

Of Oskar Schindler, Pantirer says, "He saved my life. He was like an angel sent from heaven."[4]

The most common form of rescue was to shelter or hide Jews. People in several countries took individuals or families into their homes. In Lithuania, the Polish nun Anna Borkowska hid Jewish resistance fighters in her convent, sometimes smuggling weapons to them in the ghetto. The famous Austrian actress Dorothea Neff shared her home and her meager food rations with a Jewish friend for three years. Father Dragutin Jesih in Croatia hid Jews in his own house. The Dutch farmer Johannes Bogaard hid dozens of Jews in rural locations on and around his farm. Jan Zabinski, engineer with the Warsaw zoo, together with his wife Antonia, sheltered Jews who were fleeing the ghetto by hiding them in empty animal cages. In Belgium, Abbe Joseph André and Father Bruno Reynders worked with the Jewish underground to find safe homes where hundreds of Jewish children waited out the war.

For most Jews, there was no safe place to hide. Some were saved by rescuers who helped them escape the lands of their torture. In southern France, the monk Marie-Benoit enabled hundreds of Jews to escape to Switzerland and Spain. Elizabeth Abegg, who taught school in Berlin before the war, helped her former Jewish students flee to Switzerland. Sergeant Hugo Armann helped Jews flee the Polish ghetto of Baranowice and supplied them with weapons. Italian clergymen Guiseppe Nicolini, Rufino Niccaci, and Aldo Brunacci gave hundreds of Jews shelter and new identities as they fled persecution.

A number of the Righteous used their positions to get Jews to safety. Angelos Evert, chief of police in Athens, Greece, issued over one hundred false credentials to Jews in that city. Paul Grüninger, police commandant for St. Gallen, Switzerland, defied official orders and permitted thousands of

Jews to enter his country. Some diplomats also disregarded orders and issued thousands of transit visas that allowed Jews to escape through their countries or neighboring nations: Aristides de Sousa Mendes, Spanish consul-general in France; Sempo Sugihara, Japanese consul-general in Lithuania. These men were punished by their governments. The Swedish diplomat Raoul Wallenberg issued thousands of transit passes that saved many of the Jews of Hungary.

Some rescuers were labeled Righteous for single acts of heroism. Major Max Liedtke ordered his soldiers to stop the SS from crossing a bridge to raid the homes of Jews in Przemysl, Poland. Sergeant Anton Schmid rescued Jews in and around the ghetto of Vilnius, Lithuania. Karolina Kmita was honored for hiding and caring for two Jewish girls in a Polish forest.

Oskar Schindler was unlike most of the other Righteous. He did not hide people; he sheltered them in the open, in full view of the SS, but out of range of their control. For Schindler's Jews, there was no place to which they could flee. They were located in the heart of the General Government, with death camps in every direction. He could not get them out as others had done; he could only keep the brutality from getting in.

Schindler did not have the ability or the authority to issue fake credentials or protective passes. But he falsified the ages of his employees so they would escape otherwise certain death. He invented jobs and classified people with skills they did not possess so they appeared to have value to the Nazis.

Oskar Schindler poses next to the tree he planted on the Avenue of the Righteous Among the Nations at Yad Vashem.

In effect, he handed out passes that enabled people to escape from the land of cruel forced-labor camps to the relative paradise of a humane factory.

Oskar Schindler was declared Righteous not for a single brave act, not for saving one, but for hundreds of small acts of heroism over a five-year period from 1940 to 1945.

Schindler and Madritsch

The uniqueness of Schindler's heroism is probably seen most clearly in comparison with a contemporary. Julius Madritsch, also declared a Righteous Gentile, operated a uniform factory very close to Schindler's Emalia. He too had a reputation for running a decent operation. Like Oskar, he provided thick soup, extra bread, and hope for his employees. He was, as one of his workers testified, "a good human being with a heart."[5]

When the invitation came to move factories into Plaszow, Schindler said *no* and Madritsch said *yes*. Although employment in the uniform factory kept Jews alive, the location inside the camp invited death. Amon Goeth or any of his SS guards could come into the factory and harass or shoot people at will. Schindler's insistence on keeping his operation out of the camp provided greater protection.

At the closing of Plaszow, Schindler acted and Madritsch remained silent. Schindler tried to talk his friend into going to Brinnlitz with him, moving his factory also. But Madritsch would not. "I've done everything I can for the Jews," he said.[6] Schindler was able to squeeze the names of some of the uniform factory workers onto his list, but the rest were sent from Plaszow to extermination centers. Madritsch saved a number of Jews, but only until August of 1944. Schindler's Jews lived through the war.

"I Couldn't Just Stand By . . ."

What is it that makes Oskar Schindler different from Julius Madritsch and so many of the other Righteous Gentiles? Perhaps it is that Schindler had two obsessions: to save as many as he could and to beat the system. For Schindler it was not enough to shelter those who came to him; he went looking for others to snatch from Nazi tyranny. It was not enough to have a war-essential business as a front. He had to make sure that business would not produce anything of value to the war effort.

What makes Oskar Schindler different from the people around him? Why did he risk his life and spend his fortune to help mistreated Jews while others did nothing? How did he overcome his inner cowardice? What changed a man once reviled as a swindler into someone adored as a father? In his own words, the answer is simple: "I hated the brutality, the sadism, and the insanity of Nazism. I just couldn't stand by and see people destroyed. I did what I could, what I had to do, what my conscience told me I must do. That's all there is to it."[7]

TIMELINE
Shaded areas indicate events in the life of Oskar Schindler

1908

April 28: Oskar Schindler born in Zwittau in Sudetenland, present-day Czech Republic.

1918

Treaty of Versailles creates country of Czechoslovakia.

1928

March 6: Schindler marries Emilie.

1933

Hitler becomes chancellor of Germany.

March 22: Concentration camp at Dachau opens.

April 26: Gestapo established.

May 10: Nazis burn banned books in public.

1934

August 2: Hitler names himself "Führer," or leader, of Germany.

May 31: Jews in Germany no longer allowed to serve in armed forces.

September 15: Anti-Jewish Nuremberg Laws are enacted; Jews are no longer considered citizens of Germany.

1935

Schindler family business goes bankrupt; father leaves mother; Schindler joins *Abwehr*.

1936

Nazis boycott Jewish-owned businesses.

March 7: Nazis occupy Rhineland.

July: Sachsenhausen concentration camp opened.

1937

July 15: Buchenwald concentration camp opens.

1938

March: Mauthausen concentration camp opens.

March 13: Germany annexes Austria and applies all anti-Jewish laws there.

July: Schindler arrested by Czech authorities for spying and sentenced to death but is not actually executed.

July 6: League of Nations holds conference on Jewish refugees at Evian, France, but no action is taken to help the refugees.

October 5: All Jewish passports must now be stamped with a red "J."

October 15: Nazi troops occupy the Sudentenland.

November 9-10: Kristallnacht, the Night of the Broken Glass; Jewish businesses and synagogues are destroyed and 30,000 Jews are sent to concentration camps.

September: At Munich Conference Sudetenland ceded to Germany.

1939

March 15: German troops march into Czechoslovakia.

1939 *(continued)*

March 15: Schindler freed from prison.

August 23: Germany and the Soviet Union sign a non-aggression pact.

September 1: Germany invades Poland, beginning World War II.

October 26: Krakow becomes capital of German-occupied Poland.

November 23: Jews in Poland are forced to wear an arm band or yellow star.

December: Schindler leases enamelware factory.

1940

April 9: Germans occupy Denmark and southern Norway.

May 7: Lodz Ghetto is established.

May 20: Auschwitz concentration camp is established.

June 22: France surrenders to Germany.

September 27: Germany, Italy, and Japan form the Axis powers.

November 16: Warsaw Ghetto is established.

1941

March 3–20: Krakow ghetto created, walled, and sealed.

June 22: In Operation Barbarossa, Germany invades the Soviet Union.

October: Auschwitz II (Birkenau) death camp is established.

1942

January 20: Wannsee Conference discusses Final Solution.

March 17: Killings begin at Belzec death camp.

May: Killings begin at Sobibor death camp.

May 28–June 8: Krakow ghetto *Aktion* deports 6,000 to Belzec death camp. Schindler witnesses ghetto *Aktion* and determines to help Jews.

June: Construction of labor camp at Plaszow begun.

July 22: Treblinka concentration camp is established.

October 27–28: Krakow ghetto *Aktion* deports 7,000 to Belzec and Auschwitz.

Summer–Winter: Mass deportations to death camps begin.

Winter–December 1943: Operation Reinhard undertaken to annihilate all Jews in central Poland.

1943

March 13–14: Krakow ghetto liquidated; 2,300 deported to Auschwitz.

Schindler builds his factory into a subcamp of Plaszow forced-labor camp.

April 19: Warsaw ghetto uprising.

Fall: Liquidation of Minsk, Vilna, and Riga ghettos.

1944

March–May: Germany occupies Hungary and begins deporting Hungarian Jews.

1944 *(continued)*

July 24: Majdanek, first concentration camp to be liberated, is liberated by Soviets.

September: Enamelware factory closed, *Schindlerjuden* taken to Plaszow.

October: List of Jews to be taken to his new camp at Brinnlitz is prepared.

November: Schindler rescues Jewish women from Auschwitz-Birkenau.

November 8: Death march of Jews from Budapest to Austria begins.

1945

January: Last prisoners in Plaszow evacuated.

January 17: Auschwitz inmates begin death march.

April 6–10: Buchenwald inmates sent on death march.

April 30: Hitler commits suicide.

May 8: Germany surrenders.

May 9: Brinnlitz camp liberated one day after end of World War II.

1949–1957

Schindler lives in Argentina.

1957

Returns to Germany.

1961–1974

Makes seventeen trips to Israel to visit *Schindlerjuden.*

1962

April 28: Named Righteous Gentile by Yad Vashem.

1974

October 9: Oskar Schindler dies in Frankfurt, West Germany.

1982

Thomas Keneally's book, originally titled *Schindler's Ark*, is published.

1993

Steven Spielberg's film *Schindler's List* debuts.

June 24: Emilie Schindler named Righteous Gentile by Yad Vashem.

2001

October 5: Emilie dies.

Chapter Notes

Introduction: A Righteous Gentile

1. Herbert Steinhouse, "The Real Oskar Schindler," *Saturday Night*, vol. 109, no. 3, April 1994, pp. 40–49. Online version, <http://www.writing.upenn.edu/~afilreis/Holocaust/steinhouse.html> (September 2, 2004).
2. Ibid.
3. Ibid.
4. Ibid.
5. Yad Vashem, "The Righteous Among the Nations," *Israel Ministry of Foreign Affairs*, n.d., <http://www.mfa.gov.il/MFA/MFAArchive/2000_2009/2003/6/the%20righteous%20among%20the%20nations> (September 3, 2004).

Chapter 1. The Adventurer

1. Emilie Schindler, *Where Light and Shadow Meet: A Memoir* (New York: W.W. Norton, 1996), p. 23.
2. Ibid., pp. 24–25.
3. Ibid., p. 26.
4. Louis Bülow, "Murray Pantirer: A Schindler Survivor," *Schindler Survivors*, n.d., <http://www.auschwitz.dk/panzuck/id2_m.htm> (September 3, 2004).
5. Elli Wohlgelernter, "Who Saved the 'Schindlerjuden?'," *Jerusalem Post*, November 10, 1999, <http://www.jpost.com/com/Archive/10.Nov.1999/Features/Article-2.html> (November 3, 2003).
6. Ibid.

Chapter 2. The Nazi

1. William L. Shirer, *The Rise and Fall of the Third Reich: A History of Nazi Germany* (Greenwich, Conn.: Simon & Schuster, 1959), p. 96.
2. Ibid., pp. 81, 95.

3. Thomas Keneally, *Schindler's List* (New York: Scribner, 1982), p. 38. Reprinted with permission of Simon & Schuster Adult Publishing Group from *Schindler's List* by Thomas Keneally. © 1982 by Serpentine Publishing Co. Pty. Ltd.; Emilie Schindler, *Where Light and Shadow Meet: A Memoir* (New York: W.W. Norton, 1996), p. 37.

4. Keneally speculated that one motivation might have been to avoid military service (p. 39). Emilie did not give a motive, but said Oskar "really liked" finding and persecuting spies (p. 30). Reprinted with permission of Simon & Schuster Adult Publishing Group from *Schindler's List* by Thomas Keneally. © 1982 by Serpentine Publishing Co. Pty. Ltd.

5. Schindler, p. 32.

6. "Schindler's 1938 Arrest as a Nazi Spy: The Proof," *David Irving's Action Report On-line*, December 12, 1999, <http://fpp.co.uk/online/99/11/Schindler5.html> (September 3, 2004).

Chapter 3. The Opportunist

1. Thomas Keneally, *Schindler's List* (New York: Scribner, 1982), p. 51. Reprinted with permission of Simon & Schuster Adult Publishing Group from *Schindler's List* by Thomas Keneally. © 1982 by Serpentine Publishing Co. Pty. Ltd.

2. In Keneally's book Amelia is called Ingrid. Reprinted with permission of Simon & Schuster Adult Publishing Group from *Schindler's List* by Thomas Keneally. © 1982 by Serpentine Publishing Co. Pty. Ltd.

3. "Leopold Page Describes Meeting Oskar Schindler," *United States Holocaust Memorial Museum*, n.d., <http://www.ushmm.org/lcmedia/viewer/wlc/testimony.php?RefId=LPS0560m> (September 3, 2004).

4. Louis Bülow, "Poldek Pfefferberg," *The Oscar Schindler Story*, n.d., <http://www.oskarschindler.com/19.htm> (September 3, 2004).

5. Before World War II, Poland had 3.3 million Jews. The General Government, the portion of Poland of which Frank was governor, had 2.5 million.

6. Bülow.

7. Elinor J. Brecher, *Schindler's Legacy: True Stories of the List Survivors* (New York: Penguin, 1994), p. 256. From *Schindler's Legacy* by Elinor Brecher. Copyright 1994 by Elinor Brecher. Reprinted by permission of the author.

8. Ibid., p. 125.

Chapter 4. The Industrialist

1. Lucy S. Dawidowicz, *The War Against the Jews, 1933–1945* (New York: Holt, Rinehart and Winston, 1975), p. 116.

2. Martin Gilbert, *The Holocaust: A History of the Jews of Europe During the Second World War* (New York: Holt, Rinehart and Winston, 1985), p. 106.

3. Herbert Steinhouse, "The Real Oskar Schindler," *Saturday Night*, vol. 109, no. 3, April 1994, pp. 40-49. Online version, <http://www.writing.upenn.edu/~afilreis/Holocaust/steinhouse.html> (September 3, 2004).

4. Ibid.

Chapter 5. *Herr Direktor*

1. "Krakow: The Ghetto," *Museum of Tolerance Multimedia Learning Center*, n.d., <http://motlc.wiesenthal.com/text/x13/xr1347.html> (September 3, 2004).

2. Louis Bülow, "Anna Duklauer Perl," *The Oscar Schindler Story*, n.d., <http://www.oskarschindler.com/3.htm> (September 3, 2004).

3. "Concerning the Sheltering of Escaping Jews," *Polish Righteous: Those Who Risked their Lives*, n.d., <http://savingjews.info/bekanntmachung3.htm> (September 3, 2004).

Chapter 6. The Protector

1. Gerald Reitlinger, *The Final Solution: The Attempt to Exterminate the Jews of Europe*, 2nd rev. and expanded ed. (New York: Thomas Yoseloff, 1961), p. 102.

2. William L. Shirer, *The Rise and Fall of the Third Reich: A History of Nazi Germany* (Greenwich, Conn.: Simon & Schuster, 1959), p. 1256.

3. Elinor J. Brecher, *Schindler's Legacy: True Stories of the List Survivors* (New York: Penguin, 1994), pp. 83–84. From *Schindler's Legacy* by Elinor Brecher. Copyright 1994 by Elinor Brecher. Reprinted by permission of the author.

4. Thomas Keneally, *Schindler's List* (New York: Scribner, 1982), p. 133. Reprinted with permission of Simon & Schuster Adult Publishing Group from *Schindler's List* by Thomas Keneally. © 1982 by Serpentine Publishing Co. Pty. Ltd.

5. Brecher, p. 385.

6. Oskar Schindler, 1964 interview, *Oskar Schindler: An Unlikely Hero*, n.d., <http://www.ushmm.org/museum/exhibit/focus/schindler/schindler.php> (September 3, 1994).

7. Brecher, pp. 261–262.

8. Ibid., p. 200.

9. Ibid., pp. 248.

10. Ibid., pp. 77–98.

11. Eric Silver, *The Book of the Just: The Unsung Heroes Who Rescued Jews from Hitler* (New York: Grove Press, 1992), p. 148.

12. Emilie Schindler, *Where Light and Shadow Meet: A Memoir* (New York: W.W. Norton, 1996), p. 59.

13. Brecher, p. 185.

14. Ibid., p. xxxii.

15. Louis Bülow, "Murray Pantirer: A Schindler Survivor," *Schindler Survivors*, n.d., <http://www.auschwitz.dk/panzuck/id2_m.htm> (September 3, 2004).

16. Brecher, pp. 1–38.

17. Herbert Steinhouse, "The Real Oskar Schindler," *Saturday Night*, vol. 109, no. 3, April 1994, pp. 40–49. Online version, <http://www.writing.upenn.edu/~afilreis/Holocaust/steinhouse.html> (September 3, 2004).

Chapter 7. The Labor Camp Operator

1. Elinor J. Brecher, *Schindler's Legacy: True Stories of the List Survivors* (New York: Penguin, 1994), pp. 350–351. From *Schindler's Legacy* by Elinor Brecher. Copyright 1994 by Elinor Brecher. Reprinted by permission of the author.

2. Elli Wohlgelernter, "Who Saved the 'Schindlerjuden'?," *Jerusalem Post*, November 10, 1999, <http://www.jpost.com/com/Archive/10.Nov.1999/Features/Article-2.html> (November 3, 2003).

3. Brecher, p. xviii.

4. "Schindler's List: The Death of One of the Last Remaining Survivors," *Tom Paine: Common Sense*, May 19, 2000 <http://www.tompaine.com/feature2.cfm/ID/3152/view/print> (September 3, 2004).

5. Brecher, p. 361.

6. Ibid., p. 90.

7. Ibid., p. 377.

8. Ibid., p. 407.

9. Ibid., pp. 39–52.

10. Ibid., p. 429.

11. Ibid., p. 91.

12. Eric Silver, *The Book of the Just: The Unsung Heroes Who Rescued Jews from Hitler* (New York: Grove Press, 1992), p. 149.

13. Brecher, p. 151.

14. Ibid., p. 187.

15. Murray Pantirer, "Describes one of Oskar Schindler's rescue efforts," *Oskar Schindler: An Unlikely Hero*, n.d., <http://www.ushmm.org/museum/exhibit/focus/schindler/schindler.php> (September 3, 2004).

16. Brecher, p. 180.

Chapter 8. The Listmaker

1. Elinor J. Brecher, *Schindler's Legacy: True Stories of the List Survivors* (New York: Penguin, 1994), p. 250. From *Schindler's Legacy* by Elinor Brecher. Copyright 1994 by Elinor Brecher. Reprinted by permission of the author.

2. Emilie Schindler, *Where Light and Shadow Meet: A Memoir* (New York: W.W. Norton, 1996), p. 65.

3. Thomas Keneally, *Schindler's List* (New York: Scribner, 1982), p. 289. Reprinted with permission of Simon & Schuster Adult Publishing Group from *Schindler's List* by Thomas Keneally. © 1982 by Serpentine Publishing Co. Pty. Ltd.

4. From translations of the following three Web sites: Mieczyslaw Pemper, "Life in the Face of Death," *Spiegel Online*, n.d., <http://www.spiegel.de/sptv/thememabend/0,1518,228272,00.html> (July 21, 2004). "Wladyslaw Bartoszewski und Mietek Pemper: Ehrenbürger der Universität Augsburg," n.d., <http://www.presse.untaugs burg.de/unip/press/up20021/artikel_10.shtml> (July 21, 2004). Christoph Paninka, "Mietek Pemper spricht über, Mut zum Widerstand,'" *Marianum Buxheim*, September 25, 2003, <http://news.marianum.ws/modules/news/article.php?storyid=5> (July 21, 2004).

5. Eric Silver, *The Book of the Just: The Unsung Heroes Who Rescued Jews from Hitler* (New York: Grove Press, 1992), p. 151.

6. Brecher, p. 115.

7. Ibid., p. 151.

8. Ibid., p. 387.

9. Keneally, p. 314.

10. "Oskar and Emilie Schindler," *Visiting Yad Vashem*, n.d., <www.yad-vashem.org.il/visiting/trees/schindler.html> (September 7, 2004).

11. Ibid.

12. Keneally, p. 330.

13. Herbert Steinhouse, "The Real Oskar Schindler," *Saturday Night*, vol. 109, no. 3, April 1994, pp. 40–49. Online version, <http://www.writing.upenn.edu/~afilreis/Holocaust/steinhouse.html> (September 2, 2004).

14. Keneally, p. 340.

15. Herbert Steinhouse, "The Real Oskar Schindler," *Saturday Night*, vol. 109, no. 3, April 1994, pp. 40–49. Online version, <http://www.writing.upenn.edu/~afilreis/Holocaust/steinhouse.html> (September 3, 2004).

16. Brecher, p. 224.

17. Schindlcr, pp. 90–91.

Chapter 9. The Displaced Person

1. Elinor J. Brecher, *Schindler's Legacy: True Stories of the List Survivors* (New York: Penguin, 1994), p. 70. From *Schindler's Legacy* by Elinor Brecher. Copyright 1994 by Elinor Brecher. Reprinted by permission of the author.

2. Ibid., pp. 53–76.

3. Thomas Keneally, *Schindler's List* (New York: Scribner, 1982), p. 368. Reprinted with permission of Simon & Schuster Adult Publishing Group from *Schindler's List* by Thomas Keneally. © 1982 by Serpentine Publishing Co. Pty. Ltd.

4. Elizabeth Gleick, "Requiem for a Hero: The Jews on Oskar Schindler's List Remember their Unlikely Savior," *People Weekly*, March 21, 1994, vol. 41, no. 10, pp. 40–46.

5. Keneally, pp. 369–371.

6. Brecher, p. 363.

7. Emilie Schindler, *Where Light and Shadow Meet: A Memoir* (New York: W.W. Norton, 1996), p. 100.

8. Toby Axelrod, "Schindler Widow Wants a Piece of the Pie," *Jewish World Review*, October 20, 1999, <http://www.jewishworldreview.com/1099/schindler1.asp> (September 7, 2004).

9. Schindler, p. 115.

10. Eric Silver, *The Book of the Just: The Unsung Heroes Who Rescued Jews from Hitler* (New York: Grove Press, 1992), p. 148.

11. Brecher, p. 296.

12. Ibid., p. 277.

13. Ibid., p. 230.

14. Silver, p. 148.

15. Louis Bülow, "Poldek Pfefferberg," *The Oscar Schindler Story*, n.d., <http://www.oskarschindler.com/19.htm> (September 3, 2004).

Chapter 10. Among the Righteous

1. Louis Bülow, "Poldek Pfefferberg," *The Oscar Schindler Story*, n.d., <http://www.oskarschindler.com/19.htm> (September 3, 2004).

2. Ibid.

3. Yad Vashem, "The Righteous Among the Nations," *Israel Ministry of Foreign Affairs*, n.d., <http://www.mfa.gov.il/MFA/MFAArchive/2000_2009/2003/6/the%20righteous%20among%20the%20nations> (September 3, 2004).

4. Elinor J. Brecher, *Schindler's Legacy: True Stories of the List Survivors* (New York: Penguin, 1994), pp. 179–195. From *Schindler's Legacy* by Elinor Brecher. Copyright 1994 by Elinor Brecher. Reprinted by permission of the author.

5. Ibid., p. 113.

6. Thomas Keneally, *Schindler's List* (New York: Scribner, 1982), pp. 290–291. Reprinted with permission of Simon & Schuster Adult Publishing Group from *Schindler's List* by Thomas Keneally. © 1982 by Serpentine Publishing Co. Pty. Ltd.

7. Louis Bülow, "Anna Duklauer Perl," *The Oscar Schindler Story*, n.d. <http://www.oskarschindler.com/3.htm> (September 3, 2004).

Glossary

(Italicized words are German.)

Aktion—German for "action." Used for operations in which Jews in the ghettos were harassed or rounded up and sent to work camps or extermination camps.

Allies—Coalition of twenty-six nations, led by the United States, Great Britain, and the Soviet Union, that fought against the Axis countries of Germany, Italy, and Japan in World War II.

anti-Semitism—Prejudice against Jewish people.

Appellplatz—Large square area of concentration camps where roll calls took place.

Aryan—Term used by Nazis to refer to people of Germanic background who were, typically, tall, blond, and blue-eyed.

black market—Term for illegal trade.

Blauschein—Blue sticker attached to a Jew's identity card that indicated that the card's holder was employed in a job essential to the German economy.

bluster—Boisterous talk of empty threats spoken in a bullying way.

chancellor—One of the highest offices in German government.

convent—Residence in which nuns live together.

crematoria—Furnaces in concentration camps in which the bodies of those killed in the camps were burned.

Einsatzgruppen—Literally "action groups." Squads or task forces of the SD that followed the German army into conquered countries, killing civilians.

en masse—In a group, altogether.

ethnic—Pertaining to a race or group of people with physical, mental, or cultural characteristics in common.

Fatherland—Term used especially by Germans to refer to one's country of origin.

Final Solution—Name used by Nazis for the attempt to rid the world of Jews by exterminating them.

General Government—German name for the part of occupied Poland that was not annexed to Germany.

Herr—German term of respect used as part of a man's name, equivalent to the English *mister*.

Holocaust—The attempt of the Nazi government of Germany to completely destroy the Jews of Europe during World War II, from 1939 to 1945.

Judenfrei—Literally, Jew-free.

Judenrein—Literally, cleansed of Jews.

Kennkarte—Identity card issued to Jews in occupied Poland.

lathe—A machine for shaping articles, usually to a round or circular form.

mark—Shortened name for the German unit of money. Before the end of World War II, the unit was a Reichsmark. After World War II it was a Deutschmark.

munitions—Weapons and ammunition needed for war.

Ordnungsdienst (OD)—Jewish police force of the ghetto.

Podgorze—Area in the southern section of Krakow that was made into the Jewish ghetto.

Reichsmark—Unit of German money from 1924 to 1945.

SD (*Sicherheitsdienst*)—Intelligence branch of the SS, under Reinhard Heydrich.

SS (*Schutzstaffel*)—A Nazi military-like policing organization under the leadership of Heinrich Himmler.

Sabbath—Day of rest observed by Jews on Saturdays.

saboteur—A person who commits sabotage, deliberately causing damage to a plan or operation.

Sadist—A person who delights in being cruel.

Schindlerjuden—Literally "Schindler's Jews," name given to people Schindler employed at his camps.

schnapps—A German liquor.

siding—A railway track by the side of the main track.

Sonderkommando—"Special squad." Detachments of the SS or *Einsatzgruppen* formed for specific purposes.

swastika—A symbol of the Nazi party consisting of a cross with arms of equal length, each bent to the right.

Talmud—Jewish writings that are commentaries and discussions on laws and other Biblical matters.

Treuhänder—Trustee. Person who operates a business in trust for the government, who actually owns the business.

wantonly—In a reckless, heartless, merciless, unjust, and unprovoked manner.

Zionism—Political movement from 1896 to 1948 to unite the Jewish people, who were then scattered amongst several nations, and settle them in Palestine in a country of their own.

Further Reading

Oskar Schindler

Brecher, Elinor J. *Schindler's Legacy: True Stories of the List Survivors*. New York: Plume, 1994.

Keneally, Thomas. *Schindler's List*. New York: Simon and Schuster, 1982.

Meltzer, Milton. "Schindler's Jews," in *Rescue: The Story of How Gentiles Saved Jews in the Holocaust*, pp. 55–67. New York: Harper Collins, 1999.

Roberts, Jeremy. *Oskar Schindler: Righteous Gentile*. New York: Rosen Publishing Group, 2001.

Schindler, Emilie. *Where Light and Shadow Meet: A Memoir*. New York: W.W. Norton, 1996.

Wukovits, John F. *Oskar Schindler*. San Diego: Lucent Books, 2003.

Zuckerman, Abraham. *A Voice in the Chorus: Memories of a Teenager Saved by Schindler*. Stamford, Conn.: Longmeadow Press, 1994.

Rescuers

Altman, Linda Jacobs. *Resisters and Rescuers: Standing Up Against the Holocaust*. Berkeley Heights, N.J.: Enslow, 2003.

Axelrod, Toby. *Rescuers Defying the Nazis: Non-Jewish Teens Who Rescued Jews*. New York: Rosen Publishing Group, 1999.

Geier, Arnold. *Heroes of the Holocaust*. New York: Berkley, 1998.

Glick, Susan. *Heroes of the Holocaust.* Farmington Hills, Mich.: Gale Group, 2002.

Paldiel, Mordacai. *Saving the Jews: Amazing Stories of Men and Women Who Defied the "Final Solution."* Rockville, Md.: Schreiber Publishing, 2000.

Sherrow, Victoria. *Righteous Gentiles.* Farmington Hills, Mich.: Gale Group, 1997.

Survivors

Giddens, Sandra. *Escape: Teens Who Escaped from the Holocaust to Freedom.* New York: Rosen, 1999.

Kustanowitz, Esther. *The Hidden Children of the Holocaust: Teens Who Hid from the Nazis.* New York: Rosen, 1999.

Paldiel, Mordecai. *Sheltering the Jews: Stories of Holocaust Survivors.* Minneapolis, Minn.: Augsburg Fortress, 1995.

Rosenberg, Maxine. *Hiding to Survive: Stories of Jewish Children Rescued from the Holocaust.* Boston: Houghton Mifflin, 1998.

Shuter, Jane. *Survivors of the Holocaust.* Portsmouth, N.H.: Heinemann, 2003.

The Holocaust (General)

Altman, Linda Jacobs. *Holocaust Ghettos,* Berkeley Heights, N.J.: Enslow, 1998.

Ayer, Eleanor H. *Firestorm Unleashed: January 1942 to June 1943.* Farmington Hills, Mich.: Gale Group, 1997.

_____. *Inferno: July 1943 to April 1945.* Farmington Hills, Mich.: Gale Group, 1997.

_____. *In the Ghettos: Teens Who Survived the Ghettos of the Holocaust.* New York: Rosen, 1999.

Boas, Jacob. *We Are Witnesses: The Diaries of Five Teenagers Who Died in the Holocaust.* Scholastic, 1996.

Chaikin, Miriam. *A Nightmare in History: The Holocaust 1933–1945.* Boston: Houghton Mifflin, 1992.

Nolan, Han. *If I Should Die Before I Wake.* San Diego, Calif.: Harcourt Brace & Company, 2003.

Rogasky, Barbara. *Smoke and Ashes: The Story of the Holocaust.* New York: Holiday House, 1988.

Wiesel, Elie. *Night.* New York: Noonday Press, 1988.

Internet Addresses

Museum of Tolerance
Simon Wiesenthal Plaza
9786 West Pico Boulevard
Los Angeles, CA
310-553-8403
<http://www.museumoftolerance.com>

United States Holocaust Memorial Museum
100 Raoul Wallenberg Place, SW
Washington, DC 20024-2126
202-488-0400
<http://www.ushmm.org>

Yad Vashem
Department of the Righteous Among the Nations
P.O. Box 3477
Jerusalem, Israel 91034
<http://www.yadvashem.org>

Index